BFI FILM CLASSICS

. . . .

Rob White
SERIES EDITOR

Edward Buscombe, Colin MacCabe, David Meeker and Markku Salmi
SERIES CONSULTANTS

Launched in 1992, BFI Film Classics is a series of books that introduces, interprets and honours 360 landmark works of world cinema. The series includes a wide range of approaches and critical styles, reflecting the diverse ways we appreciate, analyse and enjoy great films.

A treasury that keeps on delivering ... any film person needs the whole collection.
Independent on Sunday

Magnificently concentrated examples of flowing freeform critical poetry.
Uncut

A formidable body of work collectively generating some fascinating insights into the evolution of cinema.
Times Higher Education Supplement

The definitive film companion essays.
Hotdog

The choice of authors is as judicious, eclectic and original as the choice of titles
Positif

Estimable.
Boston Globe

The series is a landmark in film criticisi
Quarterly Review of Film and Video

Well written, impeccably researched and beautifully presented ... as a publishing venture, it is difficult to fault.
Film Ireland

D1297420

BFI FILM
CLASSICS

MODERN TIMES

· · · · · · · · · · · · · · · · · ·

Joan Mellen

bfi Publishing

First published in 2006 by the
BRITISH FILM INSTITUTE
21 Stephen Street, London W1T 1LN

The British Film Institute
promotes greater understanding
and appreciation of, and
access to, film and moving image
culture in the UK.

British Library Cataloguing-in-Publication Data
A catalogue record for this book is available from the British Library

ISBN 1–84457–122–X

Series design by
Andrew Barron & Collis Clements Associates

Typeset in Fournier and Franklin Gothic by
D R Bungay Associates, Burghfield, Berks

Printed in Great Britain by Cromwell Press, Trowbridge, Wiltshire

CONTENTS

. . . .

I THE LITTLE FELLOW

One day in 1914, acting in *Auto Races*, a Mack Sennett Keystone comedy, twenty-four-year-old Charles Chaplin suddenly appeared in costume as a tramp, the persona that at once so endeared him to moviegoers that he became the most famous person in the world. His 'little fellow', as Chaplin described his alter ego in his 1964 *Autobiography*, was based on 'contradiction'. Chaplin, famously, along with Arthur Stanley Jefferson (Stan Laurel), had honed his comedy at Fred Karno's Fun Factory slapstick comedy company. Incorporating stock figures long a part of the English music hall tradition, Chaplin explored the incongruity and inherent absurdity of class distinctions.

From late nineteenth and early twentieth-century music halls, originally a form of working-class entertainment, Chaplin derived his persona. Out of the juggling, cycling, dancing, stilt walking, magic and other specialty acts, out of the stock characters of the late nineteenth-century music halls, the Drunkard, the Pest, the Rowdy and, indeed, the Bum, Chaplin created the utterly unique figure of his Tramp. Like the music hall comedian, he created a distinctive costume for the Tramp: not the ubiquitous striped suit, but his own variation, an outfit befitting his acknowledgment of that original working-class audience.

If the tramp's pants were baggy, his coat was too tight and pulled at the seams. If his derby was small, his weather-beaten shoes, the fronts pointed precariously upward, were several sizes too large; he walked forward but his toes pointed ever outward. A small black 'toothbrush' moustache (French critic André Bazin would describe it as a 'trapezoid') 'add [ed] age without hiding my expression', Chaplin remembered.

Kid Auto Races at Venice (Henry Lehrman, 1914); Fred Karno's Fun Factory

The tramp is small, five foot four inches tall, and a scant 125 pounds (the 'Wanted' poster in *The Pilgrim*, 1923, so describes him), with small hands and feet. His eyebrows are thick and dark. His eyes are blue, appearing very light on screen; they are outlined in black, setting them deep within his skull, to convey abiding sorrow. He substitutes wit and ingenuity for physical prowess. In *The Pilgrim*, as an escaped convict disguised as a minister, he preaches on the story of 'David and Goliath', the mythic underpinning of all of Chaplin's films. The tramp was Chaplin as he was physically, and as he might have been socially had he not been gifted with extraordinary talent as a comedian, a dancer, a pantomime artist, an acrobat and a musician.

His creation was 'many-sided', Chaplin said, 'a tramp, a gentleman, a poet, a dreamer, a lonely fellow, always hopeful of romance and adventure ... not above picking up cigarette butts or robbing a baby of its candy'. Hounded by the authorities in an endless often hilarious series of chases in which he was outnumbered by bullies twice his size, kicking his pursuer in the rear end was often his best and only defence. If the occasion warranted, Chaplin admitted, 'he will kick a lady in the rear – but only in extreme anger'. The titles of *The Idle Class* (1921) refer to him as a 'lonely tramp', matching, however, the no less 'lonely' rich wife and husband.

Innocence humanises the tramp, not least at the close of *The Pilgrim* where he cannot grasp that the marshal is setting him free to pursue his fortunes in Mexico. Far from providing sanctuary, Mexico is yet another venue of murder, mayhem and blazing guns, a mirror image of the United States. The tramp is defiant in his optimism in *City Lights* (1931) where he tells the millionaire, ironically the person who is bent on suicide, as opposed to the starving Charlie, 'tomorrow the birds will sing'.

An inherent sense of dignity does not permit the Little Fellow to view himself as weak or inferior – with rare exceptions, such as in the ending of *Sunnyside* (1919), where, defeated, he resorts to fantasy. He is never vindictive and refuses to acknowledge that he is being insulted. When people ignore him, he tips his hat.

Chivalry defines the tramp. He remains, as Chaplin said, a romantic who, for a time, in each of the films believes he will win the girl – (*Sunnyside*, *The Circus* (1928), *City Lights* – because he bears generosity and a good heart. 'He wears an air of romantic hunger',

Chaplin told Mack Sennett, 'forever seeking romance, but his feet won't let him'.

Hope accompanies the tramp, expressing the director's endorsement of his goodness, nowhere more profoundly than in the New Year's Eve dinner he arranges in *The Gold Rush* (1925). The guests, pretty young women who would never consider him an appropriate conquest, fail to appear. Chaplin has the 'lone prospector' wind up a millionaire who wins the girl, even before she learns he is rich.

The unconvincing happy endings of *The Kid* (1921) and *The Gold Rush* notwithstanding, most of the time the tramp ends up on the outside. In *The Circus*, he gives up the girl he loves to the tightrope walker, the man she desires. Then he departs, a lonely figure heading to nowhere in the opposite direction of the circus train. He does not resort to self-pity, but remains, always, an indomitable Everyman whose ingenuity, good heart and kindness are their own form of transcendence and must often be his only reward in an inhumane society. Nor is the tramp even always kind: in *Shanghaied* (1915) he shanghais men into service with a sledge hammer before he's shanghaied himself. It's the director who's compassionate: the tramp too often can't afford to be.

Nothing is more important in the Chaplin films than employment, which precedes love and the possibility of domestic tranquillity, and here Chaplin reveals his most marked advance from the music hall stereotypes from which his tramp derives. Unlike the figures of English vaudeville, Chaplin places his Everyman within the economic structure of a faltering social order.

If a 'New Mission' appears in the final shot of *Easy Street* (1917), the poor now suddenly transformed into well-dressed, well-behaved citizens, the *mise en scène* subtly attributes this change not to religion, but to a sign that has suddenly appeared on Easy Street: 'Employment Agency'. Working, having enough to eat, lifts mankind out of a moral chaos created by poverty, Chaplin suggests.

The tramp may be a farm labourer (*Sunnyside*); an inmate (*The Pilgrim*, 1923); an escaped convict (*The Adventurer*, 1917); an 'immigrant' (1917); a war recruit (*Shoulder Arms*, 1918); a janitor in a bank (*The Bank*, 1915); a 'shanghaied sailor' (*Shanghaied*); a day labourer (*Work*, 1915; *Pay Day*, 1922); a waiter (*The Rink*, 1916); a street musician (*The Vagabond*, 1916); or, in *Modern Times* (1936), a factory worker, a construction worker, a night watchman, a mechanic's apprentice and a waiter. These are the venues to which his poverty carries him. He remains, always, a fortuitous step away from homelessness and starvation. Eating is paramount in the Chaplin film because the tramp never has enough to eat. Yet there is no idealisation of labour, in keeping with an aesthetic of socialist realism. When the men have the choice of 'sewer work' or working in a brewery in *A Dog's Life* (1918), every one of them chooses the brewery.

Chaplin goes further in his exploration of the ethos of work. He suggests that work and exploitation are synonymous. Chaplin developed this theme early on, in *Work* where the worker must pull up a steep incline a cart piled up with ladders, paint cans and other equipment, as well as his reclining overweight boss; the boss whips him all the while as if he were an animal. Charlie is a worker, but he's dressed as the tramp, and he does most of the work, while his boss sits on a table smoking a cigarette and barking out orders.

'Oh, my silver!' says the wife of the house, glancing at both of them and then securing her valuables in a safe.

Unimpressed, Charlie collects his boss's watch and his own. Then he zips them up into one of his pockets, as if it were just as likely that the woman would steal – from them. Under such conditions, no work gets

Work: an exploited worker and middle-class mayhem

done; the boss winds up with a bucket of paint over his head, the stove blows up, shots are fired and mayhem reigns. In *Pay Day*, Charlie is a construction worker who is cheated out of his overtime pay. When he complains, the foreman steals an additional bill from his pay envelope as soon as he's sufficiently distracted.

In *Easy Street*, the poor are violent and vicious; endlessly they exploit each other, like the thief preying on his fellow passengers in *The Immigrant* (1917). Chaplin does not idealise the poor, any more than he does labour. Invariably 'hungry and broke', the Little Fellow becomes the prey of bullies, the impoverished denizens of Easy Street. He confronts the most virulent of these as a derelict-turned-policeman. Charlie's values always intact, whatever his circumstances, he remains socialistic, handing back a stolen ham to a pathetic woman suffering from malnutrition, an affliction suffered by Chaplin's own mother. That the tramp has metamorphosed into a policeman in uniform does not prevent him from stealing vegetables to accompany the ham.

In the affluent society, to which Chaplin points in *mise en scènes* filled with shiny new automobiles and fashionably dressed people, the tramp remains on the outside, his cane and derby pleading for the respectability he will not be granted, despite his inherent chivalry and good nature. Deep focus places the tramp in the foreground while, behind him, particularly in *City Lights*, the city moves at its intransigent, self-satisfied pace. The tramp is the little man, who goes unnoticed, as the unemployed were disregarded in a ruthless social order. Chaplin suggests that upward mobility is a phantasm given the present social configuration.

. . . .

Social inequality is the premise of all the tramp films, with the tramp on the wrong side of the class divide. Yet the tramp retains his capacity for kindness. Indigent as he is, he finally takes in the abandoned baby in *The Kid*. In direct contrast to the Little Fellow, the rich are callous, arbitrary and capricious, if only because they can be. The millionaire in *City Lights*, whose life Charlie saves, recognises him only when he is under the influence of alcohol. Drunk, he embraces the tramp. Sober, he has his butler throw the Little Fellow back out onto the street, over and over again. The humour lies in the brutal and irredeemable consistency of the rich, Chaplin's technique, deriving indeed from the music hall tradition, residing in the well-timed repetitions.

By such inhuman treatment, expecting little more, the Little Fellow is bemused. Yet he also cannot erase his yearning. The famous final close-up of *City Lights* – where the tramp awaits a response from the blind flower girl, whose sight has been restored as the result of his efforts, and who sees at last the face of her benefactor – is heartbreakingly ambiguous. Her gratitude, like that of the girl in *The Circus*, does not herald a happy ending for the tramp. Chaplin quickly closes the film, sparing the spectator the agony of witnessing the tramp's rejection by the woman toward whose well-being he has invested everything of himself, all that he has, all that he is.

Images of suffering suffuse Chaplin's films, although visual gags invariably preclude the maudlin. In *The Immigrant* the shaking shoulders of the tramp as he leans over the side of the ship turn out to reveal not that he is vomiting, but that he has caught a fish. So too the shaking torso of the alcoholic husband in *The Idle Class* denotes not his remorse, but that he has been shaking up his next round of cocktails. The rich are neither different nor better than the poor, and the striped pyjamas the tramp wears as a guest of the rich in *The Adventurer* are virtually identical to those he wore as an inmate.

City Lights: 'Tomorrow the birds will sing'

A variation on the gag that blurs the distinction between rich and poor, between things as they are and things as they seem, occurs in *The Bank*. Looking quite the dandy, the tramp ambles down the street, enters the bank and opens the safe, only to emerge with a mop and bucket; he's not a bank clerk, but the janitor. Nor here in this early Essanay two-reeler does the tramp revere the rich: Charlie requests of a rich man in a top hat that he stick out his tongue and lick a stamp. The 'rich' swell, soon to mastermind a bank robbery, complies.

In Chaplin's films, the rich are allied to the police; a rich man pays off the police and so drives unimpeded through the intersection in *A Day's Pleasure* (1922), while middle-class Charlie remains mired in tar. Because he is clever, he does manage to extricate himself from the scene, driving away with his little family, while the two fat bullying cops remain stuck in the tar of their greed and self-righteousness.

In *The Idle Class* the rich are miserable, alcoholic and, as always, heartless. Whenever they have the opportunity, the rich exploit working people; the property men in *The Circus* are denied their back pay; the circus owner pays a pittance to the tramp, concealing the fact that he's the hit of the show, and that the sizable audience is a consequence of his performances. The owner is not concerned about the possibility of the tramp falling to his death from the tightrope because he has had him 'insured'.

. . . .

Even more astonishing was that Chaplin continued to depict the horrors of poverty and the brutality of class distinctions in an America whose democratic principles had been under assault by the Palmer Raids of 1918–21, precursors of Senator Joseph McCarthy's move to power through accusations that citizens were Communists, and by definition disloyal to their country.

Woodrow Wilson's Attorney General, A. Mitchell Palmer, conducted illegal searches and raids on the headquarters of unions and socialist organisations. In the wake of several bombings, Palmer declared that the Communists were about to overthrow the United States government, the excuse he gave for arresting without warrants and holding without trial workers whose only crime was that they belonged to the International Workers of the World (IWW). In his defence of the right of business to ignore the demands of organised workers, by any

means to hand, Palmer was aided by a special assistant, twenty-five-year-old John Edgar Hoover, who was soon to become the lifelong nemesis of Charles Chaplin. Palmer's agents seized resident aliens and succeeded in deporting several hundred supposed enemies of the state, among them anarchists like Emma Goldman.

No dissenter was safe as the press inflamed public opinion, promoting fear of terrorism. In 1919, Congress refused to seat a socialist representative from Wisconsin, Victor L. Berger, because he had evinced pacifist views during World War I. Berger was sentenced to twenty years in prison for sedition before his conviction was thrown out by the United States Supreme Court.

Ignoring that he was working in the midst of a 'Red Scare', financially independent Chaplin did not censor himself. He portrayed his Little Fellow as a victim of capitalist exploitation and as the frequent target of a terrorist police force. In many of the films – including *Modern Times* – he is shot at. Only his balletic abilities keep him safe, as in *Pay Day* where, enlisting the unlikeliest of body parts, he catches bricks tossed up to him by fellow workers. Chaplin was never a realist, nor did he intend to be. The tramp survives because he has the kinetic energy of someone with nothing to lose, a resilience symbolised by his acrobatics.

If the Little Fellow is a victim, however, he is no radical. In *Shoulder Arms*, he joins the war effort willingly, eager to do his part, while the director, beyond the political limitations of his character, exposes the mindless cruelties of war. In *Easy Street*, as a freezing, starving, homeless derelict, albeit after considerable hesitation, the Little Fellow joins the police force. The omnipresence in his films of a larger social consciousness separates Chaplin the auteur from his character, and reveals the distance Chaplin moved from his origins in English vaudeville.

The tramp is earnest; Chaplin is ironic. The tramp fearlessly ventures out onto a tightrope in *The Circus*, claiming, 'I have a charmed life'. The director knows otherwise, as police emerge from every doorway, threatening the tramp, nowhere more blatantly than in *A Dog's Life*. That Chaplin believes in the ultimate victory of social justice is conveyed in the tramp's solidarity with those less fortunate (like the abused girl in *The Circus*), and in his endless capacity for survival.

Chaplin believed that the 'theme of life is conflict and pain', and recalled years later that 'all my clowning was based on this'. His comedy, following the most conventional of plot formulations, involved 'the process of getting people in and out of trouble'. Humour best served these troubling themes, Chaplin believed, because it 'heightens our sense of survival and preserves our sanity ... because of humour we are less overwhelmed by the vicissitudes of life'.

The origins of Chaplin's screen persona, as Chaplin himself noted, may be discerned in his Dickensian childhood. In his self-invention as the tramp who survives, even as he continues to suffer the abuses of capitalist society, Chaplin repeatedly re-enacted his own tumultuous early life. He dramatised how today's working man too easily becomes tomorrow's homeless tramp, the opening conceit of *Modern Times*. *The Kid* was no less autobiographical, the grown-up orphan rescuing his own small self.

. . . .

Charles Spencer Chaplin was born on 16 April 1889 into what he was to call 'the poorest class in England, with no past, nor castles nor ancestors to defend'. The irony was unmistakable. His vaudeville artist father had abandoned his mother the year after his birth; hunger stalked them. At the age of five, when his mother, a musical comedy artist, suddenly lost her voice – for good – Charles Chaplin appeared on stage for the first time to complete her act, to the delight of the audience. He was a natural entertainer.

Living in dark garret rooms, Charlie, his mother and his older brother Sydney moved through hard times. Briefly, Charlie attended school, wearing his mother's cut-down red tights for socks so that the other children laughed and called him 'Sir Francis Drake'. Soon Hannah Chaplin gave up and took her sons to live, first in the Lambeth workhouse, and then outside London at the Hanswell Schools for Orphans and Destitute Children. There Charlie lived for two years, from the ages of five to seven. He had already imbibed the idea that 'poverty was a crime'. He was discharged on 10 March 1896.

In 1898, Charlie and his brother lived with Chaplin senior and a disagreeable mistress for about two months. Chaplin was to recall that at the age of nine he had been set to scrubbing the floors by his father's lover. As Parker Tyler puts it in Chaplin: *Last of the Clowns*, 'Charlie inherits his father's shoes too early and had to wear them too early. If he can't find love, it is less a consequence of physical ungainliness as the world's recalcitrance'. Chaplin senior died in 1901.

In his *Autobiography*, Chaplin locates childhood influences on his comedy, among them the amusement of watching a sheep escape from the local slaughterhouse, an incident that turned into the horror of its capture. This established, he wrote, 'the premise of my future films – the combination of the tragic and the comic'.

At eight, he joined a group of clog dancers called the 'Eight Lancashire Lads', whose repertoire included acting out the parts of characters from the novels of Dickens. On one occasion, he stole a scene in a pantomime of a dog by adding scatological details. With his mother, the victim of a psychological disarray brought on by malnutrition, now in and out of mental asylums, and his brother Sydney in the Merchant Marine, Chaplin took on a number of jobs to survive.

At times in his childhood, he lived alone. On the road with the troupe, he was frequently put up in a boarding house where he knew no one. 'The interim of one year seemed a lifetime of travail', he wrote later. He was, among other things, 'a layer-on for a Wharfedale printing machine' which he thought 'was going to devour me'. The origin of the voracious, ruthless machines in *Modern Times* reflected a childhood experience. He took pictures of people in the street with a five-shilling camera and tried to sell them in penny cardboard frames. He had yet to learn to read.

Chaplin's films reveal him to be the most graceful of dancers. By the age of twelve, he was earning five shillings a week giving dancing lessons. He was also a natural in music and managed, without being able to notate music, to learn violin and cello. When he was nineteen and performing in Paris, Claude Debussy told him, 'you are instinctively a musician and a dancer', words he would remember all his life. The great Nijinsky told him, 'your comedy is balletique, you are a dancer'.

Charles Chaplin was a quick study and, landing in Hollywood, he recognised immediately that financial independence alone would grant him the freedom to pursue this fledgling art form. At one point, he pleaded with one of his employers, First National, for an additional $10–15,000 a picture. 'I might as well have been a lone factory worker asking General Motors for a raise,' he would say later. He argued that the funding, paltry as it was, would allow him 'to keep up the standard of my work'. When his request was turned down, United Artists came into being.

As a man, Chaplin bore the psychological scars of his childhood. He pursued women in their teens, small, vulnerable girls who would, hopefully, be grateful; sometimes he provided them with opportunities in his pictures. In his fifties, Charles Chaplin married the eighteen-year-old daughter of Eugene O'Neill. Then he settled into the comforts of domesticity the Little Fellow craves in so many of the films, from the two-reelers to the tramp's final appearance in *Modern Times*.

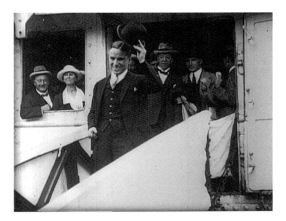

Chaplin on his first world tour caught by the *Topical Budget* newsreel in 1922: he drew huge crowds everywhere, was universally beloved

An acquaintance named Thomas Burke described Chaplin as 'a man of querulous outlook, self-centered, moody, and vaguely dissatisfied with life', a 'hard, bright icy creature', inconsiderate, and 'a born solitary'. Yet, Burke noted as well, Chaplin was a man of contradictions, because he could also be 'as kind and tender as any man could be'.

Burke believed he had discovered another contradiction. While Chaplin enjoyed the 'best of the current social system ... at heart he is the reddest of Red'. Instinctively egalitarian, and a socialist, his political instinct was to support all the little fellows of the world.

Bolshevism did attract him, like so many artists of his time. In 1922, when he visited Europe, reporters asked if he was a Bolshevik. Chaplin said he was not. Lenin, he added, was 'expressing a new idea'. Charles Chaplin, emerging from grinding poverty, who was rescued only by the miracle of his exceptional talent, and by the burgeoning success of Hollywood and the motion picture, could not help but take an interest.

Upon his return to America, Chaplin published a book called *My Trip Abroad* (1922). He pondered 'the unemployment problem' and lamented that in his films he had not done enough to address social conditions, with the exception of his anti-war film, *Shoulder Arms*. His aim in the great films that followed was to trace a route out of misery, a hellish existence of deprivation of which he was reminded on his visit to England when he encountered an old, homeless blind man he

remembered from his youth. This man, he was to write, was 'the personification of poverty at its worst, sunk in that inertia that comes of lost hope'.

Chaplin knew that those born into poverty, as he had been, had 'scarcely any chance at all'. In his life he enjoyed yachts and chauffeurs – and his own private tennis court illuminated by night, and where he played every day, even as he called tennis 'dance'. His swimming pool was constructed in the shape of the inside outline of the tramp's derby.

In his art, Chaplin turned the blinding light of his sympathy on the suffering he might so easily have himself further endured had not exceptional talent – indeed, genius – been his. Chaplin's respect for the poor is epitomised in his creation of the tramp, even as his 'other self', Chaplin the man, might on occasion don a silk hat and hobnob with peers of the realm.

Chaplin's overriding theme is that everyone should share the 'best of the current social system', that none be denied comfort and pleasure, so that his enjoyment of the wealth and fame his films brought him proves to be no contradiction at all. The political views that suffuse all his

Shoulder Arms: Chaplin excoriates war; his character attempts to fulfil his obligation

films – with their dissidence, their distrust of the state, symbolised by the endless supply of vindictive policemen – came not from the Communist Party, as J. Edgar Hoover would have preferred to prove, but from his own life experience. The exigencies of the 1929 Depression that plunged thousands into ready-waiting poverty, only reinforced views Chaplin had long held.

He sought out the great men of his time: H. G. Wells, Albert Einstein, George Bernard Shaw and Mahatma Gandhi, with whom he discussed socialism. Although he was no longer one of them, Chaplin insisted that he remained drawn to 'poor, humble people'. His films confirm his sincerity. He was an auto-didact, compiling a serious library at his home in Beverly Hills that included a book H. G. Wells recommended called *Economic Democracy*.

In the early 1920s, the pointless cruelty of prisons disturbed him. Upon his return to America from that first triumphant return to Europe, in the company of writer Frank Harris, he visited Sing Sing prison in New York State. The cells must have been 'built by a monster or a maniac', Chaplin wrote. 'I'd go mad there', he added, a sentiment he would dramatise in *Modern Times* where he portrays the factory as a prison, complete with heavy gates and police to herd the workers to their fate. He wrote that prisons should be abolished: 'Call them hospitals and treat the prisoners as patients', he urged. From personal experience he knew that 'crime is the outcome of society'.

In the aftermath of World War I, Chaplin endorsed 'universal peace, war never striding through the world again'. He did not pretend to be an expert. He was an artist, and among the inventors of the art of cinema. Critics of the highest stature, like André Bazin, respected his artistry. 'Chaplin needed the medium of the cinema to free comedy completely from the limits of space and time imposed by the stage or the circus arena,' Bazin was to write. Chaplin was a thoughtful, melancholic man, and a keen observer whose political views reflected the lonely road he had travelled out of poverty.

The travail of Chaplin's childhood never left him, even as, in his own words, his psychology was shaped by 'cold, hunger and the shame of poverty'. One day in 1942, a very famous man now, he was playing doubles at a lunch party on the North Fork of Long Island, New York. More than fifty years old, he proved to be a poor sport. Sergei Eisenstein, who made Chaplin's acquaintance on his ill-fated visit to Hollywood,

Chaplin with Sergei
Eisenstein in Hollywood:
'*Potemkin* ... the best
film in the world'

would recall that Chaplin was unable to laugh at himself when in a party
game he was given a low rating (a four out of ten) by the other guests
when it came to sense of humour.

When he began to lose that game of tennis, Chaplin threw down
his racket. Then, casually, he went over and picked it up, twirling it as if it
were the tramp's cane. Soon he was strutting around the court mimicking
the Little Fellow's duck walk. To the chagrin of the other players, one of
whom was future publishing genius Roger Straus, Jr., the small audience
of observers immediately lost any interest they might have had in the
tennis. On that afternoon, Chaplin, attending with his friend Will
Durant, was not pleased to discover himself in the company of the
daughter of French fascist Pierre Laval.

The incident duplicates an evening party at Chaplin's home, more
than a decade earlier, where he entertained Eisenstein and his

collaborators, Grigori Alexandrov and Edouard Tisse. The other guests included the great Spanish director Luis Buñuel and writer Eduardo Ugarto. Neither could speak English, according to Ivor Montagu, in *With Eisenstein in Hollywood*. They did speak French. Whatever the linguistic exigencies, the conversation eluded Chaplin, who soon began to clown, dancing an exotic routine to the radio, and impersonating the King of Siam. At one point Chaplin confided that William Randolph Hearst's mistress Marion Davies was 'his one and only real, long-lasting love'.

Ever insecure, needing still to prove himself, despite his extraordinary success, Chaplin demanded centre stage even among friends and his own guests. Turning losing into regaining the centre of attention on that tennis court, he recapitulated the trajectory of his life where he began with neither education nor prospects, neither fortune nor family, only to emerge as an artist of such unique distinction and appeal that no matter where he travelled, as if he were the Pied Piper of Hamelin, crowds followed in his wake.

No twentieth-century artist was to reveal more sympathy for the poor and the outcast, for the working man. Chaplin offered not pity for the 'little fellow', but admiration for this ordinary man with his endless capacity to survive, for his energy, fortitude, integrity, generosity and humanity. The Little Fellow remains a person without malice, no matter the abuse inflicted upon him by bullies, the rich and their hired hands, the police. Each of the Chaplin films with the Little Fellow at its centre concludes in a spiritual victory.

. . . .

Chaplin became the great cinema poet of the Depression with *City Lights*, *Modern Times* and *The Great Dictator* (1940), a trilogy dramatising the effect on the ordinary man of the global economic collapse. *Modern Times* would offer the American film its first realistic images of America under economic siege, unemployed workers filling the streets, perpetual strikes, the starvation of those crowded out of the economy and heart-rending Hoovervilles.

The Great Dictator connects the Depression with the rise of the Nazis. Chaplin defied the British, who threatened to ban the film should he make it, and the Jewish producers who urged him to desist because such a film could only further inflame the Nazis and anger Hitler. Chaplin replied that Hitler couldn't be any worse than he was.

Encouragement issued from Franklin Roosevelt, who told Chaplin he personally would ensure that *The Great Dictator* was distributed. American Communists refrained dutifully from criticising Hitler during the period of the Hitler–Stalin pact. But Chaplin took no orders from Moscow when it came to his art – or his politics – and went ahead anyway. Defiantly he ignored the Communist Party line urging 'peace' during the period of the pact.

In *The Great Dictator*, as in *Modern Times*, workers complain about the inhumane conditions of their existence, with the difference that in the later film they are promptly arrested and shot. At the end of this, his first sound film, Chaplin reveals he has something to say. Rejecting an aesthetic that, even at such a moment of urgency, forbids the didactic, Charles Chaplin the man steps out of character to address his audience.

Decrying the 'machines' that 'have left us in want', no more here than in *Modern Times* does he blame the 'machine age' for the world's troubles. Rather, it is those who own the machines, taking little notice of his needs, who have threatened the very survival of the Little Fellow. It is they who have permitted the rise of fascism.

II TOWARD *MODERN TIMES*

In 1931, following the opening of *City Lights*, Chaplin embarked on his second world tour, one that kept him abroad for eighteen months and offered him first-hand experience of the long tentacles of the Depression. 'Unemployment is the vital question,' Chaplin said, adding that machinery 'should benefit mankind ... not throw men out of work'. He spoke as if he were living in a world where freedom of speech was a sacred right. 'If capital represents the genius of America, it would seem obvious that for its own sake the present conditions should not continue or ever again be repeated,' he declared. He called for 'some radical change to cope with these conditions'. Carefully, he added that his criticisms were directed toward a return to 'stability'.

'The world at the moment is in such turmoil of change,' he told Flora Merrill of the *New York World* in February of 1931, 'that there are no signs of stability anywhere on which to speculate sensibly concerning the future.' Reporters constantly sought his political opinions, and Chaplin saw no reason not to oblige. 'Patriotism is the greatest insanity the world has ever suffered,' he remarked. Predicting another war, he added, 'I hope they send the old men to the front the next time, for it is the old men who are the real criminals in Europe today.'

He was disturbed by the rise of nationalism, defining himself as an internationalist, and remarking, 'I am incapable of a fervent love of homeland, for it has only to turn Nazi and I would leave it without compunction.' He said that a more equitable distribution of wealth was the economic solution to the Depression.

At a London dinner hosted by Lady Astor, he responded to a question posed to all the guests. What would they do to help England 'if given the power of a Mussolini'? Chaplin replied that he would first reduce the size of the government. He would control prices, interest and profits. He would amalgamate England's colonies 'into an economic unity'. He would abolish the gold standard, something Franklin Roosevelt went on to do.

His sympathies were always with the working man. Chaplin added he would reduce the hours of labour and provide a 'comfortable amount' of money to all men and women over twenty-one. He insisted that 'the well-being of the majority' had to be balanced against the freedom of private enterprise. He was quoted as warning that neither Gandhis nor Lenins fomented revolutions. Rather, mass movements, indeed revolutions, were 'forced up by the masses and usually voice the want of the people'.

Endlessly curious, he met with Gandhi, who argued that industrialising had made India dependent upon England. Chaplin knew better than to blame technology for the inequities of the social order. If

Chaplin with Mahatma Ghandi in England: India would 'sooner or later … adopt machinery'

machinery is used altruistically, he told Gandhi, 'it should help to release man from the bondage of slavery, and give him shorter hours and time to improve his mind and enjoy life'. It was 'machinery with only the consideration of profit' that had 'thrown men out of work and created a great deal of misery'. He predicted that India 'sooner or later' would 'adopt machinery'.

Chaplin's critics frequently misunderstood his attitude toward industrialisation. 'If it weren't for the machine age, the movie camera would never have been invented,' Louis Goldblatt, a CIO (Congress of Industrial Organizations) organiser, told him.

'I wish it hadn't,' an irritated Chaplin rejoined.

Chaplin himself had survived the 1929 crash financially solvent. Noting in 1928 that millions were unemployed, he had cashed in his stocks and bonds, enduring criticism from people like Irving Berlin, who accused him of 'selling America short' and being 'unpatriotic'. In 1932, Chaplin claimed a net worth of about $8 million. That 5 million people were out of work in the richest country in the world infuriated him. 'It seems impossible to believe ten million people wanting when so much real wealth is evident,' he wrote in a five-part series of articles published upon his return from Europe in *Woman's Home Companion* (1933–4).

'I am reputedly a comedian, but after seeing the financial conditions of the world I have decided I am as much an economist as financiers are comedians,' Chaplin said. 'People everywhere want more material benefits and the privileges that go with wealth. Financiers will have to take less profit and they will have to get on a basis of greater volume of business and smaller return.' His use of the imperative suggests not only naiveté, but that man who had operated from childhood as if he had nothing to lose. Chaplin recognised that the business world 'stands resolute against any fundamental change in the capitalistic system which might cheapen money and facilitate the means of buying those cheap goods.'

The dole was 'the saving grace' of England, Chaplin said in 1933. In Berlin, he met Albert Einstein, whose son told Chaplin that he was popular 'because you are understood by the masses', the reverse of his father. Together, Chaplin and Einstein lamented the Depression and growing unemployment, discussing automation and its effects on labour, themes that would surface in *Modern Times*. If new industries like the automobile and the radio had aided the labour movement, since those days the need for manpower has been rapidly decreasing because of modern machinery,' Chaplin concluded. New enterprises would not 'require the manpower that was necessary in the past'.

Chaplin closed his *Woman's Home Companion* series with a paean to his adopted homeland: 'Somehow I feel that in America lies the hope of the whole world. For whatever takes place in the transition of this epoch-making time, America will be equal to it.'

Chaplin attributed his interest in socialism, his belief that politics was in fact 'an economic problem', to his acquaintance with Upton Sinclair, whose 1934 candidacy for governor of California he supported. Sinclair talked about putting 'the state into making pictures', promising to 'ask Charlie Chaplin to run part of the show'.

Already distrusting the press, Chaplin made certain to distance his films from politics. 'I am always suspicious of a picture with a message,' he had told Flora Merrill. 'Don't say that I'm a propagandist.' Then he confided that 'as I grow older I find it is better to go with the tide'. *Modern Times* would reveal that accepting the status quo, and hoping for survival, was not a viable option for society's expendable people.

In the early 30s, left-wing critics attacked Chaplin for not going far enough politically. He was chastised for failing to predict in his films a socialist revolution in America, and for failing to speak on behalf of such a revolution himself. Pointing out how exploitation undermined a worker's sanity was not sufficient, Chaplin's Communist critics argued. Harry Alan Potamkin went after Chaplin in a flurry of magazines from *New Freeman* to *Hound and Horn* to *Creative Art* to *Close Up*.

Chaplin had been 'frustrated', Potamkin wrote, 'in part by the cultist stress placed upon his achievement, but mainly by the environment in which he is active', as if Chaplin could have worked anywhere but in Hollywood. Potamkin disliked *City Lights* because it abandoned its 'main theme of social satire – the relation between the millionaire and the classic hobo – to the minor sentimental motif of the blind girl'. Chaplin's 'quasi-intellectuality hindered him', Potamkin thought, suggesting that Chaplin betrayed his art by fostering, indeed encouraging, a personal legend of himself.

From Mexico, in 1934 Lorenzo Turrent Rozas wrote an article called 'Charlie Chaplin's Decline'. Praising *The Gold Rush* as 'one of the harshest criticisms ever made of capitalism in its last stage', Rozas, like Potamkin, attacked *City Lights* for its romantic ending. Once a director who had exposed 'the injustices of a regime', who 'with his laughter' had 'shaped projectiles to hurl at the squat edifice of capitalism, at the unjust society that inhabits it', Rozas lamented, Chaplin had wound up in 'sterile negation'.

Instead of endorsing the revolution that would ameliorate the evils he depicted, Chaplin had assumed a futile anarchist position, Rozas thought. With *City Lights*, Chaplin 'gave the impression that the social organisation that [he] criticised would endure'. He had become 'an accomplice of capitalism', and this was not to be forgiven. Bitterly, resorting to an *ad hominem* argument, Rozas suggested that Chaplin had chosen this path because he was unwilling 'to throw away the ballast of his millions'.

Years later, in his *Autobiography*, without mentioning Rozas by name, but clearly referring to his article, Chaplin admitted that he had been 'depressed' by these charges. 'I found myself agreeing with him,' Chaplin said. His next film was *Modern Times* which he would make, as he had long made all his films, free of the studio system and answerable to no bankers or industrialists. He was free to expose the contradictions within capitalism, to accept the challenge of his critics.

. . . .

Chaplin began work on the scenario for *Modern Times*, which would be his first film in five years, aboard his new yacht *Panacea*, which he purchased in 1931. The first announcement for *Modern Times* came in August 1933. Chaplin confided to the press that the film 'will be laid in the lower part of any big city with factories'. In 1934, the Chaplin studio announced that this would be the first time Mr Chaplin would 'shoot' from a manuscript completed beforehand. Up to that point he had contented himself with beginning with only the skeleton of a story in hand, and then improvising on the set.

Until 1935, *Modern Times* was called, officially, 'Production No. 5'. United Artists denied a report that the new film would be called *The Street Waif*. For a while, Chaplin thought *Commonwealth* would be a strong, ironic title, with its implied challenge toward what kind of commonwealth it could be that took so little notice of the common weal.

Chaplin also considered the title *The Masses*, one he borrowed from the name of the socialist magazine of which his friend Max Eastman had been the editor. *The Masses* had ceased publication after its editors were indicted in 1917 under the Espionage Act for publishing material that undermined the war effort. Among the cartoonists working for *The Masses* had been one George Bellows, whose name Chaplin apparently borrowed mischievously for the tortuous feeding machine of *Modern Times*.

Early notes for *Modern Times* available in the Chaplin archives reveal an original scenario with more violent themes of revolutionary upheaval than the film would finally embrace: 'shot in factory, men pull machine apart. Men could conspire to destroy the machine. They put me to work for the purpose, but I am innocent of their plan. A drama of communism and everybody getting two cars.'

Even in this version, which heralds the beginnings of a revolution where workers reject the status quo and take action, the tramp would play his role as Everyman, standing in for a spectator who needed to be convinced that things were as bad as they obviously were. *Modern Times* would be a 'satire on the factory system', Chaplin said.

Most of Chaplin's press statements during the years of production, however, were devoid of political content. They were bland and provided more gossip than insight into the startling film to come. He talked about how he put $1 million of his own money into the production. (*Modern Times* would eventually cost $2 million.) He described the factory and department store sets being constructed at the Chaplin studios: the interior of the power plant's moving machinery was to be made of wood and rubber, but painted to look like steel; the factory would be fully a block long and several storeys high. He described the subject of the film as 'a humble worker in a high-pressure factory' so that when he drops a nut to scratch himself, the entire factory is upset.

Chaplin made no mention of the fact that the factory owner is depicted in the film as spying on the workers through a gigantic television screen. He would not confide that this capitalist would bear a striking physical resemblance to Henry Ford who, having invented the American assembly line, had called on the army to disperse striking workers. Chaplin had visited Ford's Detroit plant in 1921.

Another announcement was issued by the Chaplin studios on 1 August 1934: 'Its locale will be the industrial quarter of a great city and its main action will be outlined against a varying background of factories, workshops, waterfronts and dance halls.' Charlie would befriend a 'waif'.

In another statement Chaplin admitted that he would be depicting a 'high-pressure factory', an employee who is fired, an arrest at a Communist parade and a 'final rally'.

A story appeared in the *New York Herald Tribune* reporting Chaplin's denial that he 'would satirize the NRA' (Roosevelt's National Recovery Act) in the film now in production. Chaplin replied that he was 'a great admirer of President Roosevelt and in entire sympathy with his policy'. Yet all those references to workers and factories alone seemed inflammatory. Chaplin protected his film and himself by arguing that he was only creating 'a comedy picture with no endeavor to comment or satirize on social or political affairs'.

Until the end of the decade, Hollywood for the most part avoided even mentioning the Depression. An overwhelming number of the films produced during the 30s were comedies featuring socialites in furs and jewels sipping highballs in elegantly appointed apartments.

Or films avoided confronting the Depression by being located in the past. When Mae West descended on Hollywood in the early 30s, she set *She Done Him Wrong* (1933) in the 1890s. Otherwise, the Depression did not exist as far as Hollywood was concerned. If there are hoboes riding the rails in Frank Capra's *It Happened One Night* (1934), they are barely noticeable; certainly Capra's hero Clark Gable, about to marry a rich woman, upward mobility intact, is not one of them. *Modern Times*, with its persistent description of how ordinary people were faring during the Depression, would be an act of enormous political courage, and Chaplin knew it.

Asked if the tramp and his love interest, the gamin, were to be rebels or victims, a question pregnant with red-baiting innuendo, Chaplin evaded the question. His main characters would be 'only two live spirits in a world of automatons', he said. He and co-star Paulette Goddard, his lover at the time, as tramp and gamin, would express 'an eternal spirit of youth and are absolutely unmoral'. There wouldn't even be any 'romance' in the relationship, he insisted. They would be 'two playmates – partners in crime, comrades, babes in the woods. We beg, borrow or steal for a living. Two joyous spirits living by their wits'.

. . . .

Shooting began in October 1934, with Chaplin producing, directing, writing, starring in and composing the music for this, the tramp's final screen appearance. Principal photography took close to a year. It had long been Chaplin's habit to shoot many thousands of feet of film only to discard much of it. (Chaplin would shoot 9,500 feet of film for *Modern Times*, using 7,500.).

During the last stages of shooting, Chaplin lived at the studio and took his meals there. By April 1935, he was confident. 'From all indications we shall have a sensational success,' Chaplin predicted.

Because of the wit, originality and enormous charm of the tramp, as well as because he resisted the advent of sound, Chaplin's abilities as a film-maker were not thoroughly appreciated neither during his own time nor later. He was fastidious as a director; his shot compositions, the intricacy of his *mise en scène* and the sharpness of his editing reveal a director of the first rank, nowhere more powerfully than in *Modern Times*.

Like Eisenstein, he compiled shot lists. The early notes for *Modern Times* include: 'large city – early morning rush of commerce – showing subway street traffic – newspaper printing office – factory whistles – ferry boats – ambulance – fire engine – modern traffic'. All this was to be contrasted with 'a comedian' with nothing to do, who has trouble crossing a road, who nearly falls down a grating outside a store window: 'different jobs and fired from each'. The firings would remain; the riffs on his trouble crossing the road and nearly falling down a grating (borrowed from *City Lights*), would not appear in the final cut. A potential gag list included the following:

Stomach rumbling
Steam shovel
Kidnapping
City environment
Museum and public gallery
Dry goods store
Street fair
Docks
Dives
Cabarets
Bank parade
Street fire
Police raid
Street riots

Strikes
Telephone wire repairing
Dock working
Baggage staircase
Labor exchange
Bread line.

There were no small number of abandoned sequences as Chaplin strove for a focused unified effect. In the rejected street-crossing scene, the tramp tries to cross against the light, only to fall into the arms of a policeman, who insists that he go back and wait until the light flashes 'go'. The crowd pushes him persistently back, so that he is able to move only when the sign says 'stop'. By the end of the sequence, the tramp walks off in frustration, having failed in his effort to cross the street. Because the scene functioned only as a set piece, without furthering the action, Chaplin let it go.

In another abandoned sequence:

Charlie would find his way into the locked room where the factory's management are experimenting with a robot which can fly an aircraft. Surprised by the bosses, Charlie is obliged to disguise himself as the robot, and must then go through the robot's actions, including flying the plane.

So explained Alf Reeves, Chaplin's press relations man, who added, 'if more thrills were required, it could be worked up with the effects mechanism they use now and it should be an incident which could be worked up for a big gag'. In another rejected idea, Charlie, in one more effort to be gainfully employed, pretends he is a qualified steam shovel operator.

In yet another discarded scene, the tramp and gamin are punished for eating eggs which had been dumped in the sea as surplus; the incident reflects Chaplin's often expressed anger during the Depression that food was being discarded while millions starved.

In another idea he rejected, the tramp and gamin take shelter in an empty house which, unknown to them, is being demolished. In yet another set piece, borrowed from *The Kid*, the gamin steals wallets and purses which the tramp then returns to their owners in the hope of receiving a reward.

Chaplin on the set of
Modern Times

Chaplin omitted a scene
of his robbers filling a
bag with silver: 'We ain't
burglars. We're hungry!'

As he worked on *Modern Times*, in keeping with Paulette Goddard's importance in his personal life, Chaplin expanded the role of the gamin. In an early draft it is the tramp who is hired by the café as a waiter; he then secures a job for the gamin, 'in blissful innocence that the place is also used as a bawdy house'. In the final version of the film, the prostitution theme is dropped and the gamin is the one who finds the tramp his job as a singing waiter.

Afterwards, Chaplin explained to a shipboard acquaintance, Jean Cocteau, why he had altered so much of *Modern Times*, rejecting so many scenes, and why he had worked so long – two years – in preparing this film. 'When I had worked a scene up to perfection, it seemed to fall from the tree,' he said. 'I shook the branches and sacrificed the best

31

episodes. They existed in their own right. I could show them separately, one by one, like my early two-reelers.' The seeming disunity was, in part, the result of his general method, as David Robinson, Chaplin's authorised biographer, explains: 'to work out each sequence in turn, alternating periods of story preparation with shooting – changing, selecting and discarding ideas as the work progressed'.

. . . .

For *Modern Times*, Chaplin did for a time consider using synchronised dialogue, by then universal in American cinema for some years. He and Goddard did sound tests. A dialogue script was even prepared. Chaplin shot a scene with synchronised dialogue in the warden's office, then didn't use it. He returned to his conviction that the tramp must remain silent. It was, Chaplin would say, 'unthinkable' that the tramp should speak since 'the first word he ever uttered would transform him into another person ... the matrix out of which he was born was as mute as the rags he wore'.

The spoken word would undercut the strengths of the pantomime artist who could, after all, express every emotion by movement and gesture. So Chaplin conveyed his loyalty to that Edwardian music hall tradition from which he had developed his comedy. Weren't the movies a 'pantomimic art', Chaplin said – confusing, perhaps, his own great talent with the nature of the genre.

For Chaplin, words spoiled the art as much as they would painting or statuary. 'We might as well have the stage', he insisted, 'there would be nothing left to the imagination'. *Modern Times* would employ 'natural sounds', from a phonograph record to a television set, auto horns, radio, an ambulance siren, cowbells, police whistles and even a rumbling stomach, but no dialogue. Technically, with no obligation to shoot at sound speed (twenty-four frames per second), Chaplin could alternate rhythms, sometimes shooting at eighteen frames.

The absence of synchronised dialogue in *Modern Times*, the tramp's silence, gains Chaplin a strong thematic resonance. That the tramp and the gamin do not speak aloud reflects the futility of language in the context of the Depression. This silence also emphasises Chaplin's persistent theme that the tramp's needs go forever unheard.

Chaplin was too great an artist to sacrifice the nuances of plot simply because his characters did not speak. The spectator can guess easily what the rich man whose roast duck dinner doesn't arrive is saying; nor would the police listen to reason were the tramp to explain aloud how he came to be waving a red flag only for a street demonstration to materialise behind him. Even in *The Great Dictator*, Chaplin's first sound film, Charlie, not as the tramp but as a 'Jewish barber', isn't given much chance to speak – until the end of the film when Charles Chaplin the auteur addresses his international audience.

. . . .

It did Chaplin no good with his political enemies when, six months before its release, *Modern Times* was embraced by Boris Shumyatsky, head of the Soyuzkino (All-Union Soviet Film Trust), which had power over the entire Soviet film industry. Shumyatsky had visited Chaplin in the summer of 1935 and claimed that Chaplin had shown him a rough cut of his new film.

In *Pravda*, Shumyatsky praised *Modern Times* for revealing 'honestly and truthfully how the American working class is carrying on the struggle against capitalism'. The theme of all Chaplin's films, Shumyatsky asserted, was 'the tragedy of the petty bourgeoisie in capitalist society'. This article was reprinted in *New Masses* in September 1935.

Modern Times, Shumyatsky elaborated, depicted a 'world of slavery, exploitation and the cold glitter of the all-powerful machines', even as, 'cautiously and cleverly, Chaplin laughs at the capitalist system of rationalization'. Shumyatsky had to admit, as Rozas had noted, that Chaplin 'does not believe in the successful outcome of this struggle'.

Shumyatsky went on to give an interview to the American Communist paper, the *Daily Worker*. Now he called *Modern Times* 'a sharp satire on the capitalist system in which he [Chaplin] derides capitalist rationalization, crisis, the decrepit morality of bourgeois society, prison and war'. He bragged that his critique had led Chaplin to make 'drastic changes', in the film, particularly in the ending so that it would reveal 'the necessity for active struggle', a distortion of what the film would become. 'We argued with Chaplin and for a long time he would not yield,' Shumyatsky declared. 'But at our departure he shook our hands firmly and said, "I am pleased we met. But this meeting will cost me many weeks of labor on my film."'

The result, Shumyatsky confided, was that it took Chaplin two and a half months to alter his film, changing the conclusion. Shumyatsky described the original ending, in which the gamin was to be a Red Cross nurse, who can no longer return to Charlie and the once-romantic world of the hobo. He in turn 'withdraws to his old joyless life, a shrunken, bent and solitary man'.

The new ending supposedly had the two meeting 'after the privations and sufferings of the war'. They decide 'to work and fight together against the "machine of time,"' a euphemism for capitalist society, and walk off, hand in hand into the 'blue distance'. The tramp emerges, Shumyatsky said, 'with the conviction that it is necessary to fight for a better life for all humanity, with a conviction of the necessity for active struggle'.

Alarmed, recognising that his survival as a film artist in the United States would not permit his being embraced by a Soviet bureaucrat, let alone one who affected having influenced the themes of his work and persuaded him to change the ending of an important film, Chaplin engaged in damage control. In December 1935 he praised the New Deal, arguing that it had prevented the rise of fascism in America. Alf Reeves denied that there was any political intent in *Modern Times*.

'The Russian story reads deep, terrible social meanings to sequences that Mr Chaplin considers funny', Reeves said. Then he added: 'I can assure you that this picture is intended as entertainment, and perhaps it might be said, too, that Mr. Chaplin's purpose in making this picture is to make money.'

Chaplin told Karl Kitchen, interviewing him for the *New York Times*, that *Modern Times* did not 'contain any political inferences'. When Kitchen wrote that Chaplin had said that the title would be *The*

Modern Times marketing campaign sans political thrust

Masses, the Chaplin studio denied it. On the eve of its opening, Chaplin described the origins of *Modern Times* in decidedly non-political terms:

> I was riding in my car one day and saw a mass of people coming out of a factory, punching timeclocks, and was overwhelmed with the knowledge that the theme note of modern times is mass production. I wondered what would happen to the progress of the mechanical age if one person decided to act like a bull in a china shop – for instance to say 'nuts' to a red light and drive on – or scream at a concert that was boring. I decided it would make a good story to take a little man and make him thumb his nose at all recognized rules and conventions.

Shumyatsky – who, back home in Stalin's Soviet Union, had made Sergei Eisenstein a particular target of cruelly persistent harassment – suffered his own predictable fate. As Ronald Bergan reveals in his 1999 biography of Eisenstein, after eight years of autocratic control of the Soviet film industry, Shumyatsky was charged with having permitted 'savage veteran spies, Trotskyite and Bukharinist agents, and hirelings of Japanese and German fascism to perform their wrecking deeds in the Soviet cinema'. He was arrested in January and then shot in July of 1938, three years after his visit to Charlie Chaplin. Shumyatsky was forty years old.

The marketing campaign for *Modern Times* made no mention of exploited workers, or Communist parades. The press book available to distributors offered suggestions, such as hiring a Chaplin lookalike to wear a sandwich board reading 'I'm back again!'. United Artists stood ready to provide banners, puzzles, a gilded Chaplin shoe, Chaplin doorknob hangers, derby hats and even *Modern Times* automobile tyre covers.

The articles provided in the press kit featured famous people paying tribute to Chaplin's genius, or caricatures of Chaplin by famous newspaper cartoonists. The sketch of Chaplin's face used for the *City Lights* advertisements was recycled. Some of the publicity included the tramp pictured with the gamin, the first time Chaplin was featured with any other performer, suggesting that, in contrast to his relationships with adolescent women of no particular distinction or ability, his personal connection with Goddard was one of respect and artistic appreciation.

. . . .

The publicity for *Modern Times* studiously ignored its thematic import, but included Goddard, a unique moment of Chaplin sharing the limelight

Modern Times was scheduled to open on 11 October 1935. Then it was postponed to 16 January. Chaplin remained dissatisfied with the ending, but particularly with the musical score, and threatened to have an entire new soundtrack recorded. The *New York Times* reported – obviously using as its source Alfred Newman, head of the UA music department and the conductor of the music for *Modern Times* – that Chaplin required that he himself be present at both the writing and the recording of the score, which took place at the United Artists recording rooms.

According to the unfavourable *Times* description, Chaplin criticised the orchestration and the way the musicians played, demanding rewrites so that 'many parts were recorded twenty or thirty times'. Newman said he had slept at the studio for five nights, working sixteen hours a day. One night Chaplin returned after dining with H. G. Wells to complain, 'I'm tired of this stalling.' Newman blew up, and walked off. That the *Times* story was motivated by opposition to Chaplin's politics is revealed in its description of the plot: 'so he took two outcasts who, no matter what happened to them, would never be able to better themselves, and he built his story around them.'

The score was completed by David Raksin, Newman's assistant, who was uneasy about continuing to work with Chaplin in Newman's absence, but did so anyway. Chaplin continued to work on every musical phrase, using 'a bit of Gershwin' in one place, a 'Puccini melody' in another. Raksin, taking it all down, worked with him sometimes twenty hours a day, even sleeping some nights on the studio floor. In the process, he lost twenty-five pounds.

Two weeks before the opening, Joseph I. Breen of the Hays office ordered six sequences deleted because of 'vulgarity'.

Modern Times opened at last on 5 February 1936. Chaplin did not attend the New York première. Those in attendance included that American-bred commissar Will Hays himself, along with Douglas Fairbanks and his son, other Hollywood stars like Gloria Swanson, Edward G. Robinson, Ginger Rogers and Anna May Wong, and theatre personalities Lee Shubert and Lillian Hellman.

When *Modern Times* was re-released in the 1970s, Charles J. Maland points out in *Chaplin and American Culture* (1989), the publicity shared the same apolitical philosophy adopted in 1936. In the *New York Times* advertisement, the tramp strides forward optimistically, with an expectant look on his face, as if he has no reason to expect defeat or failure, hardly the theme of this film. Decades after the appearance of *Modern Times*, critics dissociated themselves from the political character of Chaplin's films, minimising the importance of their strong socialist underpinnings. Vincent Canby wrote in the *Times* that Chaplin's films were 'to some extent emotional autobiographies ... despite the overlay of social consciousness', as if the two were mutually exclusive. Andrew Sarris went further in an illogical attempt to depoliticize *Modern Times*, insisting that 'the solipsism of his conceptions negated the social implications of his ideas'.

The New York première of *Modern Times*: a major cultural event

III THE FILM
. . . .

Modern Times, which Chaplin called 'an American story', remains unique for its naturalistic and concrete images of an America under economic siege. The plot is an accumulation of episodes, picaresque in spirit, not a random collection of two-reelers, 'which might have been called The Shop, The Jailbird, The Watchman and The Singing Waiter', as Otis Ferguson would suggest in the *New Republic*.

Each sequence joins a progression of deepening contradictions with symmetry binding the episodes. As Parker Tyler recognised, *Modern Times* was in fact the first of the Chaplin films with a complex plot, with a pattern tending toward the epic.

The police are ubiquitous in *Modern Times*. Sometimes they are in uniform, sometimes in plain clothes. In each episode the tramp confronts the authorities, who exercise complete control over his economic well-being. A recognisable pattern soon emerges. At the close of each sequence, police close in to enforce the social order as a paddy wagon pulls up to cart the tramp off to hospital or, more frequently, to jail.

The opening title warns the spectator: *Modern Times* would be 'a story of industry, of individual enterprise, of humanity crusading in the pursuit of happiness'. Chaplin indulges his penchant for irony by invoking the 'Declaration of Independence' at the beginning of a film where the main character is enslaved.

When *Modern Times* opens, the tramp is fully integrated into the workforce. He is a labourer on the assembly line of 'Electro Steel Corp', as Chaplin reveals how tramps come into being: the economic condition of the working class turns out to be as precarious as that of the lumpen proletariat, people who survive by odd jobs and by their wits, like the tramp in *City Lights*. A tramp, Chaplin suggests, is a fired worker.

For a split second, before any music rises, a mammoth clock engulfs the shot. It is in extreme close-up so that half the numbers drop out of the frame. The clock spills beyond its perimeters as time is to dominate the worker's daily life. The clock continues under the credits where, once more, Chaplin's characters have been too dehumanised to be granted names. Charlie is 'a factory worker', defined by his social role; the nature of his work and his subjugation to it are controlled by time. Goddard is 'a gamin'. They represent not just themselves, but all members of their class.

Workers as sheep:
Chaplin as influenced
by Eisenstein

39

The clock is replaced by a shot of a herd of sheep, a black sheep among them; the sheep engulf the shot. Chaplin then dissolves to a shot of men emerging from an underground subway. It is a homage to Eisenstein's *Strike* where shots of striking workers are juxtaposed with cattle enduring their slaughterhouse fate. Chaplin had greeted *The Battleship Potemkin* in 1926 as 'the best film in the world'. When he met Eisenstein in Hollywood, he added, 'in five years it hasn't aged a bit; still the same!'. Eisenstein in turn had in 1922 praised Chaplin as having 'taken the eighth seat in the council of muses'. In 1930, Eisenstein pronounced Chaplin 'the most interesting person in Hollywood'.

Chaplin's montage, suggesting that men need not behave like sheep, implies no less a call to arms than Eisenstein's appeal to Russian workers: if men have been dehumanised, reduced to being part of a herd of animals under the control of others, might it not be incumbent on them to reclaim their manhood by taking control of their destiny? Chaplin extends the conceit with a montage of short takes and dissolves to the gated factory: like sheep, the men move from subway to street to factory, where they are locked inside its prison-like structure.

In such an environment, there can be no synchronised dialogue because the noisy machines drown out people's voices, even as the workers on the assembly line have no say in their destinies. In these images of alienated labour, neither the workers nor the spectator even know what product is being produced, as in *Metropolis* (1927) Fritz Lang's classic depiction of the dehumanisation of the worker .

The factory owner is a Henry Ford lookalike

Disembodied voices emerge on the soundtrack through machines. The video-phone through which the President of Electro Steel (Allan Garcia) issues his increasing commands to a shirtless worker manning an oversized machine – 'speed her up!' – also evokes *Metropolis*. The President uses his video-phone to harass his workers, depriving them of all privacy. His video machine even follows them to the toilet, in images predicting George Orwell's depiction of Big Brother in *1984*. Machines replace people. On a gramophone record, an engineer describes how the Bellows Feeding Machine works.

The boss is portrayed not only as cruel, but as mindless. When he is not attempting to squeeze every last drop of energy from the workers, he attempts to do a jigsaw puzzle; when this proves too challenging, he reads the comics, with 'Tarzan' facing the spectator. His uselessness is matched by his inanity.

Charlie appears at the rapidly moving assembly line, a not-unwilling cog in the machine of 'progress'. A bee buzzes in his face, but he has no leisure to brush it aside, lest some bolts he must tighten escape from his wrench. His contorted effort to distract the bee earns him a hit in the head by the club-carrying foreman who strikes, ostensibly to swat the bee; violence attaches to the simplest of moments at this factory, and those whose role it is to control the workers come armed.

The President's demands for 'more speed' have turned Charlie into a robot, someone full of tics, the machine having robbed him of his normal human rhythms. In response, Charlie exacts small rebellions. Casually he

Chaplin prefigures
Orwell's *Big Brother*

41

files his fingernails with a tool before he returns to work, like the exploited worker in Chaplin's first foray into this theme in the Essanay short, *Work*.

Chaplin deliberately renders his tramp-as-worker compliant – knowing how much he needs his job, the tramp attempts to do as he is asked. The alienation of labour is dramatised in every one of Chaplin's scenes of people working. As satire exaggerates in the service of truth, the 'factory worker' has to punch a time clock in *Modern Times* even when he goes to the bathroom where the boss discovers him smoking: 'Hey! Quit stalling! Get back to work!'

Being treated as if he were a machine causes the worker to lose control of his body. The factory worker is soon so disoriented that he sits down on his neighbour's plate of soup; then he shakes so much, as if he had been occupied by the machine, that he does spill the entire plate of soup on his fellow worker. In their effort to keep up with the demand on their labour, the workers are set against each other as competitors and antagonists.

Chaplin's 'Bellows' mechanical feeding machine, into which the factory worker is locked, is as dark an attack on the dehumanisation of labour as anything in *Metropolis*. The aim, with the 'automaton soup plate', automatic pusher and 'hydro-compressed, sterilized mouth wiper' is to eliminate the lunch hour. Electro Steel must move 'ahead of your competitor', the President is told. To help accomplish this end, the worker must eat while expending 'no energy', since all energy must be placed in the service of creating the mysterious product, one as opaque as the undefined manufactured object in Henry James's *The Ambassadors*.

The tramp has brought a lunch box so small it could barely hold a sandwich. He acquiesces in participating in the feeding machine demonstration. In deep focus his fellow workers sit on benches observing. The scene illustrates Chaplin's genius for expressing the tragic and the comic simultaneously: what begins as hilarious becomes a paradigm of the tramp's dire social condition. (Chaplin manipulated the feeding machine himself for this scene.)

The comedy derives as well from contrast, the collision of opposites. At first the machine lives up to the scientists' claims. Having allowed the worker appropriate time to eat his food, the sterile mouth wiper jauntily swings over. An extreme close-up of an ear of corn then heralds the coming disaster. As the corn suddenly begins to move violently from side to side, eating becomes an assault. While the tramp is

tortured, treated as part of an experiment rather than as a human being, the conceit is heightened by the bureaucrats, oblivious to his pain, discussing what is going wrong with the machine.

The disaster intensifies with the line, 'we'll start with the soup again'. The soup spills first onto Charlie's chest, then, a second time, into his face, hitting a technician in the eye. No one cares, even when the machine inadvertently serves the worker not only the cut-up bites of food, but the machine bolts that the hapless scientist inadvertently placed on the food tray. The whipped cream in the face gag recalls slapstick out of the early two-reelers, only for the spectator to be pulled up short when the sterile mouth wiper goes berserk. It attacks the tramp viciously and so unrelentingly that he falls out of the frame. 'It isn't practical' is the line that punctuates the scene, as if what counted was the well-being not of the worker, but of the machine.

Late afternoon finds the boss ordering that the assembly line speed up to 'the limit'. It is now that the worker is swallowed up by the machine.

Top: the 'Bellows' mechanical feeding machine; above: the 'factory worker' dehumanised as a cog in the machine finds his sanity in jeopardy

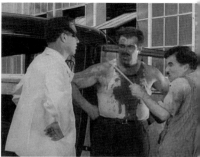

Gracefully Charlie moves along the gears, his agility that of a man half his age (he was forty-seven). By the end of the day, the tramp has gone mad, chasing a secretary to tighten the buttons on her skirt, and rushing outside where he assaults a buxom middle-aged woman with big decorative buttons adorning her ample chest. This woman is rescued by a passing policeman, underlining the theme that the police exist to preserve the economic arrangements of capitalism. Even fleeing from the police, the disoriented factory worker has been sufficiently programmed so that he remembers to punch his time card.

'He's crazy', says one of the workers. Before he has done, Charlie has pulled every lever, creating chaos in an anarchist's ballet. The President's viewing machine has become disabled. With an oil sprayer in his hand, Charlie gives his pursuers a merry chase in what might be seen as a homage to the role of the chase in the silent film. The chase, as Siegfried Kracauer wrote in his *Theory of Film*, fulfils the natural tendency in cinema for endless motion.

Marrying ballet with the acrobatic, as Chaplin often did, the tramp swings up to the ceiling. This ballet is spontaneous and original and unpredictable, in counterpoint to the regular rhythm of the assembly line. Sound is allied to action as the acrobatic flight is punctuated by the siren sound of the arriving ambulance. Before he is carted off to a mental hospital, however, the tramp manages to spray oil into the eyes of both a policeman and the ambulance driver.

The culmination of the extraordinary opening sequence of *Modern Times*, in which an ambulance transports the tramp to a mental hospital, Chaplin wrote in his *Autobiography*, derived from his having heard of healthy young men off the farms who after four or five years on the Detroit assembly lines turned into 'nervous wrecks'. The tramp has suffered what was then called a 'nervous breakdown'.

A skillful ellipsis reveals a white-haired doctor urging the worker to begin 'life anew', and 'avoid excitement'. Then, with no further concern for his patient, he turns to flirt with a nurse, washing his hands of any further involvement with Charlie, whom he has pronounced 'cured'.

Chaplin then offers another brilliant montage, as the doctor's words collide with the street turmoil, the chaotic world in upheaval that the tramp must re-enter. Canted frames, short takes, streets filled with people angrily milling about, a society in disarray, is hardly a place where a man without power can 'avoid excitement'. Chaplin makes the point entirely without dialogue, as the great Soviet film-makers of the silent era would have done.

The point is enhanced in the factory worker's having departed from the hospital dressed as the tramp. Chaplin dramatises visually how easily a worker can descend into the ranks of the jobless and homeless. The unemployed are as ubiquitous in this film as the police hired to keep order in a society where people are out of work and starving, their plight conveyed sympathetically in Chaplin's use of canted frames.

Workers are forever scattering before oncoming police as the two groups share the streets. Chaplin's *mise en scène* reflects a world inhospitable to ordinary people with signs reading 'Private' and 'Keep Out'. A sign at the waterfront reads 'No fishing'.

. . . .

The factory worker emerging from medical incarceration as the tramp

The fired factory worker, having become a tramp, inadvertently leads a demonstration

A close-up of a flag at the back of a moving truck introduces the next scene. A red flag, signifying danger, falls off. Ever helpful, the tramp picks it up and calls out to the truck driver, waving the flag to gain his attention. In these precarious times, such a gesture is a call to arms. Behind Charlie waving the flag materialises a swelling demonstration of the unemployed, carrying signs that read 'Libertad', 'Unite' and 'Liberty or Death'.

Inadvertently, the tramp finds himself leading a revolutionary demonstration. That he didn't have to organise it, that the protest march was already in progress, underlines Chaplin's point that during the Depression spontaneous manifestations of their plight by the disenfranchised were inevitable and growing. There are, Chaplin suggests, strikers, demonstrators, around every corner.

Unemployed himself, the tramp does not acknowledge his solidarity with the rest of the unemployed. He is that Chaplin Everyman, desiring not revolution, but a decent life. His need is for survival, his motive self-preservation, not any desire to be a political organiser. So Chaplin declares that revolutionaries seek not power or personal advantage, but the daily necessities of life.

Charlie hides in a manhole, still clutching the inflammatory red flag as the police apprehend him. 'So you're the leader ...'. Despite his denials, he is carted off to prison. Police sirens punctuate the scene, as the primary sound in this film is that of authority closing in on the unprotected and vulnerable.

As he borrowed from Eisenstein, so Chaplin had learned from D. W. Griffith, who had been a founding partner, along with Douglas

Fairbanks and Mary Pickford, in United Artists. Using parallel action, Chaplin cuts to scenes now of the tramp's counterpart, the gamin (Paulette Goddard). On the first day of shooting, Goddard had appeared on the set looking glamorous in an elaborate hairstyle; Chaplin dumped a bucket of water over her head and smeared dirt along her cheek. The gamin makes her entrance, a knife between her teeth, stealing bananas on the waterfront to feed her hungry siblings; their father is among the unemployed.

Behind her in the shot, factories steam, as business as usual proceeds. Chaplin was careful to use close-ups only for maximum emotional effect, and then in relatively long takes, as in the close-up of the father in the next scene, brushing his hair back. The gesture conveys his pain at the plight of his starving children.

Paulette Goddard as the gamin: co-star and co-equal

Meanwhile the tramp is in prison, being 'held as a communist leader'. The use of the lower case in the intertitles must have been intended: Chaplin's point is that the tramp is being accused not of subscribing to Soviet politics, but of a socialism that insists upon an economic equality. He is not, as Chaplin was not, following the dictates of a foreign government.

In the prison scenes, the whistles of the guards punctuate the movements of the silent prisoners. His tramp attire gone, Charlie is dressed in a fresh new jacket and pants, as Chaplin makes the point, again visually, that the conditions of life of an inmate are better than those of an unemployed worker. As the men in the factory were turned against each other, so too in the prison, Charlie must battle his cell-mate over a place to sit, and then over a hunk of bread.

'It's mine!', the man says, as Chaplin shows how unselfishness resides no more among the outcast than between workers and bosses. In prison too drugs make their appearance. The tramp declines the offer of a palliative from a fellow inmate whom an iris shot has singled out as the suspected smuggler.

Chaplin sets up the next gag when the smuggler gets rid of the cocaine by pouring it into a salt shaker. In *Modern Times* the gags are not gratuitous set pieces designed for the demands of slapstick, but function thematically and to animate the plot. Drugs are the natural companion of incarcerated people, Chaplin suggests.

Charlie, predictably, sprinkles the cocaine-filled salt shaker over his food. His eyes widen, as Chaplin enlists his extraordinary abilities in

The factory worker, now an inmate, discovers cocaine

pantomime, here to express the effect of the cocaine. Facial expressions, widened eyes, arched eyebrows, pursed lips, twisted nose – all are enlisted to express his heightened state. Now he stares down the bully who has denied him the bread, and then takes action. The 'nose powder' has rendered him even more aggressive than his former burly antagonist. The tramp seizes the bread and then marches defiantly off to his cell.

The cocaine high lands him outside rather than in. When three inmates with escape on their minds lock the warden and guards into a cell, the tramp is available to help them. He is no rebel, no revolutionary. The ballet of his intoxication culminates in his dancing back to the cell, and confronting the rebels. Under the influence of the cocaine, he is oblivious even when they shoot a pistol directly at him, as gunshots, not for the last time in the film, echo on the soundtrack. Persistently the tramp has allied himself with the prevailing order, not least in this dance where he rescues the police.

In yet another use of parallel action, Chaplin returns to the streets where there is 'trouble with the unemployed'. A full shot of defiant, homeless men in a crowd is followed by gunshots. The gamin's father falls dead in what is called a 'food riot'. Now 'the law takes charge of the orphans', as the gamin's two sisters are hauled away by the police, two in plain clothes, one in uniform. The gamin escapes. The fade that closes each sequence lends to the structure of *Modern Times* a downward spiral of defeat.

An ironic title finds the tramp 'happy in his comfortable cell'. A

The factory worker's cell as his only safe haven – presiding is Abraham Lincoln, as Chaplin infuses the tramp with patriotism

sign on the wall reads: 'Home, sweet home'. There is a vase of flowers. Birds chirp on the soundtrack in this mockery of domesticity. On the wall of his cell is a photograph not of Marx, Lenin or Stalin, but of Abraham Lincoln, as persistently Chaplin employs symbolism, decrying realism as 'often artificial, phony, prosaic and dull'. Lincoln's image fulfils Chaplin's insistence that *Modern Times* is, indeed, an 'American story'.

In a morally and economically bankrupt society, Chaplin's hero can find tranquillity only in prison, although the director offers him no more personal identity here than he had as 'a factory worker'; in prison he is known as 'number seven'. The tramp reads a newspaper with a banner headline reading 'Strikes and Riots'. 'Breadlines' and 'unruly mobs' await him outside, and so he is not pleased when via a radio message the tramp discovers that he has been pardoned for his noble deed of rescuing the warden and guards.

Chaplin does not depart from the prison sequence without the weekly visit of a minister and his wife. The scene is not gratuitous. It is a Chaplin riff on the ineffectuality, the lack of humanity of organised religion. The stern judgmental minister's wife sitting beside Charlie shows him neither interest nor kindness. A parched figure in a dark hat, dark-framed glasses and black gloves, the woman has nothing to say to the tramp. She turns frame left away from him, as the tramp, reading a newspaper, is turned frame right.

The minister's wife continues to read her newspaper, even as her stomach begins to rumble (Chaplin created the noise by blowing bubbles

Hypocritical religion devoid of compassion: Charlie encounters a minister's wife

in a pail of water). Ever chivalrous, attempting to ignore the indelicacy, the tramp flips on the radio, only for a voice to shout, 'if you are suffering from gastritis …'. He shuts it off, quickly, in yet another display of Chaplin's unerring comic timing. The point of the scene is that religion, no more here than in *Easy Street*, offers no solace to the downtrodden. The woman's silence is another justification for the absence of synchronised dialogue in *Modern Times*.

'Well, you're a free man', the warden says in another irony, as Chaplin reveals that without food and shelter 'freedom' is meaningless. The tramp begs to 'stay a little longer', insisting that he is 'so happy here'. If the tramp seems child-like, the point is that capitalism, depriving the worker of agency, infantilises anyone who is rendered dependent. In such a society the little man may come to resemble a child, but it is the society that has rendered him helpless and unable to take care of himself. When the tramp has the opportunity, as with the gamin in the department store sequence, he reveals that he knows how to take care of another person.

Unskilled, uneducated, the most ordinary of men, the tramp is ill suited for Depression America. The warden's injunction that he 'make good', equivalent to the doctor's absurd injunction that he 'avoid excitement', is meaningless. The warden's written recommendation that the tramp is 'an honest and trustworthy man' affords him scant assistance. At a shipyard construction site, dressed as the tramp once more, as an unskilled labourer he is destined for disaster.

Yet the tramp continues to believe in a natural equality of men. Ready to work, he tries to hand his jacket to the foreman on the job. Why shouldn't his superior take his jacket? The foreman rebuffs him, as realism demands that he would. The tramp is given what seems like a simple task. He must find a wedge 'like this'. Attempting to fulfill the absurd task, the tramp can discover only the wedge that secures a half-finished ship. As soon as he lifts it, the ship sets sail, then sinks abruptly into the sea. The tramp leaves before he can be fired.

The next scene opens with a pan from a bread company truck to the gamin. Images of privilege constantly appear in Chaplin's street scenes: the Globe Theater stands across the street, contrasting the world of the haves with the empty existences of the have-nots. 'Alone and hungry', the gamin steals the proverbial loaf of bread from the back of the truck. A richly dressed woman, passing, turns her in, only for the tramp, who

The tramp's innate generosity: a final moment of compassion before he's carted off once more to prison

arrives fortuitously on the scene, to assume responsibility for this 'crime'. His desire is to return to the safety of prison anyway.

'I did it,' he says. Oblivious to the ragged girl's plight, the rich woman persists and sets the police straight: 'It was not the man. It was the girl.' *Modern Times* calls for compassion by exposing its absence.

A wipe takes Charlie to a cafeteria where he piles two trays with food, sits down and consumes every bite. Using visual means alone, Chaplin conveys the abiding physical hunger of his character. The tramp summons a policeman to him, casually utilising a toothpick on his way out. As they pass a news-stand, in yet another superb visual gag, the tramp grabs a cigar, which the proprietor obligingly lights for him, unaware that the tramp is handcuffed to the policeman, who has not yet entered the frame. With no fear of being caught, incarceration preferable to attempting to survive outside, and showing a compassion the other characters lack, the tramp then passes out chocolate bars from the news-stand to hovering hungry children.

In the paddy wagon he wrinkles his nose, a pantomime reflecting the unwholesome scent of the poor. Coincidence – never a concern for Chaplin who, whenever he could, eschewed simple realism – brings him back in contact with the gamin, to whom he offers his handkerchief and his seat. The paddy wagon swerves and sends them flying into the street, along with a policeman whom the tramp dispatches with a quick blow to the head.

The fantasy sequence that follows is preceded by a billboard in the background of the shot. It reveals once more the disparity between rich and poor: 'New Ford V-8 For 1935'. Soon the gamin confesses to the tramp that her home is 'nowhere'. Observing a scene of a worker husband going off with a lunch box while his aproned wife waves goodbye, Chaplin's tramp and gamin reveal their dream. It is one where they live as husband and wife too, not amid great wealth, but an ordinary life where their needs are met.

'Can you imagine us in a little home like that?' the tramp says. Despite Chaplin's disclaimer that there would be 'no romance' in their relationship, in the final version of the film they are much more than just 'babes in the woods', 'as Chaplin had put it. Their relationship is chaste and respectful, but it transcends his suggestion that they are mere 'playmates'.

As Griffith had done, Chaplin dramatises the fantasy of his characters. A dissolve allows the spectator to distinguish the 'real' from the imagined. Charlie is wearing overalls, like the worker whom they had just observed, reiterating that he has no desire to be anything more than a working man. A bread box suggests that their dream is as much about having enough to eat as it is about envying or appropriating the wealth of others: the tramp is not a socialist or Communist. He plucks an orange from a tree outside their middle-class home; a bird sings in a cage, an icon of lower-middle-class respectability. A cow obligingly stops at the kitchen door to provide milk for their breakfast.

Charlie plucks a grape from a vine, and then he and the gamin sit down to eat. The dissolve back to the present locates the tramp in pantomime, cutting the imaginary meat of his fantasy in a match on action. The return to the present is accompanied as well by a pan to the

Fantasy as palliative: the tramp imagines domestic tranquillity

The tramp discovers joy in imagining an existence free of want

gamin whose hunger has been intensified by the fantasy, as fantasy will inevitably collide with reality.

'I'll do it. We'll get a home even if I have to work for it!' the tramp declares in a line that is funny and true. Work is not idealised as a good in itself, nor in *Modern Times* is there any hope held out that working conditions might become more favourable in any near future. The feet of a policeman have entered the frame, as the law disperses even fantasies. The fade to black provides further deflation.

Yet Chaplin repeatedly counterpoises defeat with victory. The fade-in is to a department store where the boss, ruthlessly, has fired the night watchman because he broke his leg. Utilising the warden's letter of recommendation a second and final time, the tramp is hired.

At once he rushes outside to admit the gamin, and the two, indeed like children, explore a world of rich food, liquor, furs, luxurious beds with satin coverlets, and even toys, the furnishings of a society of plenty. The tramp guides the gamin to the lunch counter sandwiches and a large coconut-covered devil's food cake. He punches once more a time clock. At the toy department, they both don roller skates.

On skates, in a marvellous set piece, Chaplin reprises his balletic ability, that emblem of the tramp's resilience. 'Work is sublimated into dance,' Parker Tyler wrote of Chaplin's use of movement, 'as though this sort of sublimation were all that made it tolerable'. In *Modern Times*, dance, with its spontaneity and originality, is placed in counterpoint to the tramp's being shuttled about, as Tyler puts it, 'like an object of manufacture'.

'Look! I can do it blindfolded!' he exults, his bravado juxtaposed with the 'Danger!' sign just beyond. Executing the one-legged corner turn Chaplin had developed in London in his music hall apprenticeship days, he skates to the edge of a precipice, courting disaster only to transcend it. Despite his twists and turns, he does not fall to his destruction, at the last moment skating away, sometimes backwards.

Chaplin's films were greeted with so much joy all over the world because the tramp, nowhere more than in this roller-skating idyll, express- es the inherent talent, beauty and dignity of people outside the privilege of the social order. Only when the gamin, fearing he will fall, tries to rescue him does he falter. In this self-reflexive scene, Chaplin also reminds the spectator – and himself – of the talent that has brought him so far.

The tramp as night watchman: the extraordinary athleticism of Charles Chaplin as an emblem of political optimism

The night watchman in solidarity with workers reduced to thievery: crime as a consequence of poverty

On the fifth floor, the gamin models ermine, as a short dolly back reveals an entire floor of gaudy furniture, not least the quilted bed in which she falls asleep. It is a parody of all those 30s' films chronicling the lives of the rich. Having tucked her in, the tramp skates flawlessly into the china department, where the visual gag is that no dishes are broken.

Three burglars have entered the store. Charlie attempts to escape back onto the escalator only for them to drag him down. Once more in this film gunshots resound. The keg of rum, visible first in the scene where the tramp brought the gamin into the store, returns, as Chaplin obeys Chekhov's dictum that a gun observed in the first act must be fired by the third. A cut discovers the gamin sleeping so soundly that she doesn't hear the gunshots.

In yet another coincidence, one of the thieves turns out to be 'Big Bill', a fellow worker from the steel mill. Chaplin's point is that crime is a consequence of poverty. 'We ain't burglars. We're hungry!' Big Bill says. The tramp is satisfied as he joins the 'thieves' in a toast with the department store's champagne, an image of the solidarity of the working class. To underline his point, Chaplin did not include a moment he had already shot in which the thieves fill a bag with silver from the store. Need has led them to defy the law, not greed.

A cut to yet another clock is followed by a time-lapsing dissolve. The store is now filled with shoppers. A fast dolly to the fabric counter prepares the spectator for the discovery of the tramp sleeping beneath the yardage. Chaplin's editing is always economical. Yet another dissolve moves the viewer to the gamin waiting outside just as the police escort the tramp into yet another paddy wagon. Enlisting the profusion of pantomime, the tramp waves her away with a quick gesture of the hand.

A title allows that it is ten days later that the tramp is released. The barefoot gamin, embracing him with the glee, indeed, of a child, pronounces that she has found them a 'home'. She takes his arm; they hold hands, as they will at the close of the film.

The gamin's 'paradise', turns out to be a shack evoking Depression Hoovervilles. 'Of course it's not Buckingham Palace', she says, as Chaplin nods in the direction of his English heritage. Inside, a table, where a pot of flowers sits tentatively, collapses to the ground. A broom handle holds up the roof. The door falls off, catapulting Charlie into a river flowing outside. A montage unified by dissolves reveals each sleeping alone chastely.

'It's not Buckingham Palace': rare Depression images in Chaplin's cinema

Chastity governs the relationship between gamin and tramp

The river gag is reiterated in the morning where the tramp, donning a bathing costume that has materialised out of nowhere, jumps into that same river only for it to be only a few inches deep; this mishap foreshadows the entire precariousness of their idyll. During the Depression, the world for those on the outside is never what it seems, but is always recalcitrant, inhospitable and often dangerous.

Nowhere in Chaplin's films is eating more persistent in the plot than in *Modern Times*, whose theme is the effect of the Depression on the ordinary American citizen. There are at least ten scenes where food is involved, reflecting Chaplin's view that the very act of eating has in these hard times become fraught with conflict and tension.

The food theme begins when the tramp in the factory spills his co-worker's soup, continues in the scene of the eating machine, and re-emerges at the jail when Charlie wrestles for a chunk of bread. The gamin steals bananas and that long, crusty loaf of bread; the tramp consumes two huge trays of food in the cafeteria; the first thing he does as a night watchman is to bring the gamin inside and feed her at the abandoned lunch counter, where the coconut cake forms the focal point of the frame.

At their Hooverville 'paradise', the gamin produces a meal, with a close-up of the frying pan allowing Chaplin to reiterate the importance of food in the lives of these characters. Tea is poured into tin cans. There is a steak, cut from a large ham. The gamin's wink permits no moral judgment on her thievery.

Two more eating scenes will follow: one in the reopened factory

The gamin has stolen their dinner: eatiing as a monumental event in Chaplin's films

and another in the café. The final ballet of *Modern Times* will feature a roast duck, although neither the gamin nor the tramp share in this feast. *Modern Times* is about the human need for work, for food, for shelter, as each sequence is motivated by the characters' attempts to seek the basic elements of survival.

'Factories reopen!' the daily newspaper blares. Men are to be put to work. 'Work at last!' the tramp exclaims. 'Now we'll get a real home!'

It does not matter – because Chaplin has little interest in realism – that the origin of the paper, like the tramp's bathing costume, is unaccounted for. Critic Charmion Von Wiegand called *Modern Times*, accurately, 'the first expressionist film of contemporary American life', noting that expressionism in art occurs most frequently at moments of social upheaval.

Wiegand pondered as well that as an aspect of Chaplin's expressionism his characters in *Modern Times* do not develop and grow psychologically. This is true. What develops in Chaplin's films, nowhere more than in *Modern Times*, is not the psyches of his characters, but how they continue to be buffeted by and thwarted by circumstance. His great subject, as James Agee put it, was 'the problem of surviving at all in such a world as this'.

A factory has materialised out of nowhere, virtually at their back door, along with a tumultuous crowd of unemployed workers straining to gain entrance at the gates. Motivated by love, the tramp pushes forward and manages to squeeze inside ahead of the others, as Chaplin reveals how workers had to compete with each other for the few jobs available.

As a mechanic's assistant, the tramp helps to repair the idle machinery. Yet another ballet begins, triggered by the mechanic's annoyed order that the tramp move the giant tool box out of his way. Soon the tool box is swallowed up by a hungry machine, tools flying everywhere. Recalling the first sequence, men are at war with machines. The tramp picks up a tool, as if to do battle with his mechanical adversary.

As it did Charlie in the opening sequence, the machine engulfs the mechanic (Chester Conklin). Its wheels turn with such ferocity that he is almost decapitated. Men are forever being attacked by the machines, the visual equivalent in *Modern Times* for the dehumanisation resulting when human need is not considered in the frantic race for profit.

A whistle sounds. The tramp leaves his boss stuck in the machine and removes a sandwich from his hat. During the lunch hour, the

The tramp as mechanic's assistant: comedy providing the optimism of political hope

electricity is turned off so that the mechanic must remain within the jaws of the machine, upside down. The next gags reprise the mechanical feeding machine scene, as Charlie attempts to feed his boss. The tramp uses a funnel smelling of oil to pour coffee into the mechanic's mouth; when this is too repellent, a roast chicken is enlisted as a substitute. In a homage to Chaplin's early years with Mack Sennett, the tramp attempts to mash a custard pie into the mechanic's mouth, diligently wiping away the excess from Conklin's nostrils.

It's a comedy, if, as Eisenstein put it, a 'fusion of laughter with tears', so the mechanic survives. As soon as he's extricated, the factory whistle sounds. Just as once more the gears begin to move, a worker arrives to order the mechanic to 'get your coat. We're on strike!' The machines at frame left are still moving as the workers stroll out the door.

A dissolve outside reveals that the newly striking workers are already being harassed by police in the pay of the factory owners and always available to wage war against the workers. The tramp is once more singled out and escorted into yet another 'police patrol' wagon. Social unrest is inevitable as long as social inequality persists.

Meanwhile, barefoot in the street, the gamin dances to the tune of a merry-go-round, recalling that Paulette Goddard at the age of fourteen had already been a Ziegfeld dancer. In a Cinderella moment, she is spotted by the owner of the 'Red Moon' café. A dissolve to a graphic match has her continue her dance inside, but wearing a spangled costume.

Chaplin as auteur: the
graphic match suggests
the transformative power
of gainful employment

A week later, for a third time, the gamin awaits the tramp outside a
police station. She is dressed this time in a straw hat adorned with daisies.
She has risen in the world, and now wears gloves and carries a little purse.
'I have a job for you!' she tells the tramp.

The café owner wonders if he can sing, as if Chaplin were about to
reply to those critics who demanded to hear his voice. Simultaneously, in
parallel action, the police sign an arrest warrant for the gamin, ironically
for 'vagrancy', no matter that she is now employed. She is accused of
'escape from juvenile officers'. In this shot, two policemen sit idly on a
bench awaiting their next assignment. In Chaplin's films, there is always
a superfluity of police.

In the final major sequence of *Modern Times* the rich are once more satirised. The tramp, now a waiter, engages in his last ballet. It begins with his becoming ensnared in a dog's leash, and culminates in the ballet of his attempting to serve flaming roast duck.

The tramp has no more identity as a singing waiter than he had as an inmate: here the number '13' adorns his jacket, the same number that defined him in *Shoulder Arms*. A tilt up to the chandelier prepares for the climax of the scene.

A stuffy, pompous rich man is angry at having to wait 'an hour for roast duck', in sharp contrast to how little the tramp has had to eat in this and the other Chaplin films, not least the leathery old boiled boot in *The Gold Rush*. The rich are no better than the machines in the first sequence; they exhibit no regard for the human being.

Waiter Charlie is swallowed up by the swaying figures on the dance floor, who include sailors in uniform. The visual gag is impeccably timed: just as the tramp finally emerges with the roast duck, the floor is filled with dancers.

He almost makes it across the room, only to be forced back into the crowd of dancers, who, oblivious, fill the frame, the roast duck dancing on the tray over their heads. At last the tramp arrives at the angry patron's table, only for the duck to have disappeared from his tray. He searches his pants. Then the maître'd' spots the duck impaled on the chandelier. The comedy plays on. Just as Charlie is about to carve the retrieved duck, an entertainer suddenly grabs it, as if it were a football, and rushes away.

The brilliance of Chaplin's shot compositions: the tramp as waiter engulfed by the self-centred rich

Swifter and more graceful than the others, Charlie rescues the duck and carries it to the goal, the waiting guest.

'I hope you can sing', the boss says. Charles Chaplin can. The tramp is prepared this time with a song about 'a pretty girl and a gay old man', flirting on the boulevard. His diamond ring is what catches her eye. It's a meaningless ditty, if one suggestive of director Chaplin's history with much younger women. As even his daughter Geraldine would remark, Chaplin as an older man fancied 'young girls'. His act is preceded by a barbershop quartet of waiters singing a racist song about 'darkies' in the unwholesome moral atmosphere of Depression America.

'I forget the words', the tramp says, and so the gamin writes them on his cuff. He prances boldly out onto the floor, and with his first expansive gesture, his arms flung out wide, the cuff flies off, never to be seen again. The tramp keeps dancing, dancing as expertly as he ever did. 'Sing! Never mind the words !' the gamin calls out in Chaplin's final reply to those who decried his refusal to make a film with synchronised dialogue.

For the first time on screen, Chaplin's voice is heard, if only in mock-Italian gibberish. To this are added a few French-sounding flourishes and a sprinkle of English words like 'taxi meter' and 'spinach'. The song may be synchronised, but it doesn't make sense. Yet, through pantomime, finger to his lips, slapping his rear end, circling his hand on his hip, moving his arms together, the tramp tells an entire story. You don't need words, Chaplin's final pantomime insists.

Words as irrelevant: the tramp sings – in gibberish

The gamin as 'Ellen Peterson', her official identity, known only to the police

'You're great! I'll give you a steady job,' the café owner says, only for the police to close in. The arrest warrant they display grants the gamin her name: 'Ellen Peterson'. That she is demonstrably no vagrant doesn't matter as the final chase begins. The plainclothes police pursue the gamin and the tramp as if they were dangerous criminals. It's a comedy and so they get away.

In the first ending Chaplin shot, the tramp is visited in the hospital where he is incarcerated following his nervous breakdown at the factory. The gamin, now a nun, visits him. Her choice of this calling had been prepared for earlier in this scenario when the tramp and gamin met a nun and the gamin is moved by 'a momentary feeling or sense of beauty'.

A discarded ending: the gamin as a nun, with religion separating the tramp and gamin forever

'She makes me want to cry,' the gamin says in this version of *Modern Times*. At the conclusion the gamin and the tramp part with sad smiles. Charlie walks down a road only for the spirit of the gamin to dance circles around him, even as he does not see her, but continues on his lonely path. It turns out, in a sudden unexpected reversal of point of view that this is the gamin's dream, from which she is awakened by the Mother Superior. The gamin 'starts, then turns and smiles wistfully at the kindly old face and together they depart into the portals of the hospital' to the final fade.

An ending departing from the point of view of the tramp to that of another character would have been a mistake, one Chaplin was not about to make. Chaplin shot this nun sequence in late May or early June of 1935. By August, he had decided to change the ending, perhaps indeed prompted by Boris Shumyatsky's reaction to the rough cut.

Modern Times ends very differently. There is no nun, no Mother Superior, no suggestion that the gamin will renounce this world. The final scene opens with a title: 'Dawn'. The irony is blatant. The fade-in is to a long empty road on a desolate landscape, the shot devoid of human habitation. No promising future beckons, no expectation that the society that has written these characters off as expendable will be reformed any time soon. There is no sentimentality in Chaplin's depiction of the life of the worker facing the crisis of capitalism that in 1929 manifested itself in a global Depression.

A pan reveals the tramp and gamin seated side by side. The tramp, returned once more to his identity as an outsider, massages his feet, revealing that he is not wearing socks. The gamin wears the straw hat and checked dress left over from the brief moment of solvency when she danced at the café.

'What's the use of trying?' the gamin says.

'Buck up. Never say die. We'll get along,' the tramp says, expressing for the final time on screen Charles Chaplin's abiding belief in the dignity and resilience of the poor. His final word, reflected as well in the title of one of the songs he wrote for this film, is 'Smile'. The gamin smiles.

Hand in hand, they saunter down the long empty road to their uncertain future. Some of his left-wing critics thought the tramp's final image should have placed him as a cog in the wheel. of the system, back on the assembly line. But Chaplin was no realist, nor did he now defer to his Communist admirers.

'Smile!' the tramp urges

Tramp and gamin leaving a ruthless, inhospitable society behind

Their backs are to us

Back lit, silhouetted against a world not of their making, the tramp, no longer alone, and the gamin, walk into the camera, as if they were about to disappear into the lens, as if they were confronting a spectator who would prefer to ignore their existence. Then in a startling cut and a discontinuity edit, in the next shot Chaplin places the camera behind them so that, independent in their dignity, they are walking away from the viewer. It is as if Chaplin were raising a curtain between his characters and the indifferent and morally hostile society that has betrayed them.

. . . .

Modern Times, a masterpiece no less today than in 1936, quickly garnered its defenders. In the *New York Times* Frank S. Nugent decreed that Chaplin had been 're-elected king of the clowns'; the *Times* referred to Chaplin as 'the World's Prodigal Son'.

More fulsome, the *Times* theatre critic, Brooks Atkinson, wrote a column about *Modern Times* describing his personal response to Chaplin as 'wholly idolatrous' ('to an idolator [*sic*] he can do no wrong'). Atkinson referred to 'the joy, pathos and sentiment' a Chaplin film arouses, as he compared Chaplin to 'Puck, Ariel and Mickey Mouse'.

Kyle Crichton, writing in *New Masses* as 'Robert Forsythe', said he 'came away stunned at the thought that such a film had been made and was being distributed'. He called *Modern Times* an 'epoch-making event', and, given the expected ideological bent of Hollywood, a 'historical event'. In *Partisan Review and Anvil*, Edward Newhouse defended Chaplin from his left-wing critic in the Sunday *Worker*, who had attacked him because the tramp secures a job 'through a letter of warm commendation given him by a sheriff because Charlie has sided with the authorities against some of his fellow boarders in jail'.

Chaplin, Newhouse writes, 'is no more an artist of the proletarian revolution than Voltaire or Swift'. He had depicted 'the most fundamental cruelties of bourgeois society. To film these things beautifully and bitterly is a contribution as important as that of Dreiser in literature'.

John Anderson, drama critic of the *New York Journal*, took the local film critics to task for what seemed to him to be their faint praise of *Modern Times*: 'all they called it was a masterpiece', he said, protesting in hyperb-'' exultation that they failed to capture 'the delirium of the picture'.

Sergei Eisenstein pronounced *Modern Times* 'the tragedy of contemporary society', suggesting that what seemed child-like in Chaplin was connected to his sense of the tramp's political powerlessness: 'for the little man in contemporary society there is no way out. Exactly the same as for the little child.'

Eisenstein placed Chaplin 'equally and firmly in the ranks of the greatest masters of the age-long struggle of Satire with Darkness', an artist in the rank of Aristophanes, Erasmus, Rabelais, Swift and Voltaire. Against 'the Goliath of fascist Baseness, Villainy and Oscurantism', Eisenstein wrote, he was 'the tiniest of Davids, Charles Spencer Chaplin from Hollywood'.

Writing in 1947, André Bazin pronounced *Modern Times* to be 'one of the best of Charlie's full-length films – perhaps the best, along with *City Lights*':

> So far from lacking unity, *Modern Times* on the contrary is the film in which the level of acting style is best maintained, controlling thus the style of the gags and even of the script. The ideological significance never impinges from without on the comic flow of the gags. It is the imperturbable logic of the latter that utterly exposed the absurdities of our society.

In a restored version, *Modern Times* was the centrepiece of the 2003 Cannes Film Festival where an empty seat, illuminated by a spotlight, paid tribute to Charles Chaplin, who had died in 1977.

IV UNITED STATES OF AMERICA *V.* CHARLES CHAPLIN

With its images of the Depression and the hopeless quandary in which it placed the American worker, *Modern Times* inspired a global attack on Charles Chaplin. The FBI (Federal Bureau of Investigation) had opened its file on Chaplin in 1922, but it wasn't only the FBI that pursued and harassed and attempted to discredit Charles Chaplin. The German film company, 'Tobis Films', which owned the rights to René Clair's 1931 *À nous la liberté*, on 26 May 1936, initiated a plagiarism suit against *Modern Times*, demanding 1.2 million francs in damages. It was a suit pursued in both France and the United States over a ten-year period with such vigour that its sincerity has to be questioned.

In what was obviously a nuisance lawsuit designed at worst to bankrupt Chaplin, and at best to distract him, Tobias charged that he had stolen from Clair the scenes on the assembly line, the image of the mechanisation of meals, and the theme of the dehumanisation of the worker. The suit was preposterous and not only because ideas cannot be copyrighted.

If anyone had been a plagiarist, it had been René Clair himself, who stole outright images from Fritz Lang's 1927 *Metropolis*. Clair has guards watching the prisoners make little wooden horses on an assembly line, just as Lang has guards scrutinising every movement of the workers in *Metropolis*. The giant factory of *À nous la liberté* resembles a prison with workers, robot-like, performing meaningless tasks, as in *Metropolis*. Clair has men marching into the factory in lines like machines, even as the men in *Metropolis* march six abreast from the day to the night shift.

The theme that 'machines will replace men' originates in cinema with *Metropolis*, as does the ubiquitous presence of police authority. The inhuman practices of industrial capitalism are strikingly dramatised in *Metropolis*. The contorted movements of the workers in *Metropolis* as they struggle to gain control over the machine seem to be an influence on Chaplin's depiction of the disoriented worker struggling to keep up with the assembly line. It appears that if Chaplin borrowed from anyone, it was from Lang far more than from Clair.

Moreover, in his depiction of the two prisoners, Louis and Emile, one to become a factory owner, both to end up as vagabonds, Clair borrows verbatim from Chaplin's depiction of his Little Fellow. All artists 'steal' from each other, embellish, enlarge and pay homage. (Lillian Hellman even taught a creative writing course at Harvard that she named 'Stealing', pointing out that great writers steal; mediocre writers imitate.)

It is the nature of art, no less than of science, to build upon what came before. While playing a rather cowardly role in the lawsuit, attempting to distance himself and refusing to sign a statement for Chaplin's lawyers, Clair did in fact admit that Chaplin had influenced his work: 'I owe him very much', he said. Then, ambiguously, Clair added that if Chaplin had borrowed anything from him, 'he has done me a great honor'. Later Clair reiterated his acknowledgment of his debt to Chaplin: 'we are all his debtors. I admire him greatly'.

Chaplin attempted to reply. He traced the origins of *Modern Times* to his 1916 plan for a film about a trip to the moon, which was to be 'a satire on progress', and include a 'feeding machine', along with a 'radioelectric hat that would register one's thoughts'. In his *Autobiography*, he writes of his days as a child working on the Wharfedale printing machine when at times he felt as if the machine 'was going to devour me'; the machine was a 'hungry brute wanting to get ahead of me'.

Modern Times derived from the aggregate of Chaplin's experience, as a man and as an artist: his boyhood powerlessness; his two-reelers that already introduced the alienation of the worker from his labour; his visit to Henry Ford's factory; even, Chaplin was to add, images from a Walt Disney film about Santa's workshop which depicted an assembly line. The theme of men being turned into machines appears in a short story Chaplin wrote called 'Rhythme', where a firing squad, hearing the word 'stop!' that would have signalled a reprieve for the ill-fated accused, fires on him anyway. Having been transformed into killing machines, they are unable to stop themselves.

As the libel suit progressed, Tobis lawyer Milton Diamond claimed that Chaplin had viewed *À nous la liberté* numerous times in 1934 and 1935. Chaplin replied that he had never seen Clair's film. Over the decade that followed, as the suit aged, a veritable Jarndyce *v.* Jarndyce, no one could ever prove that he had. Alastair Cooke had told him about the film in the summer of 1934, Chaplin said, even as he had considered giving Cooke a small role in *Modern Times.*

A projectionist who had worked at Chaplin's studio, whose credibility was questionable, testified that he had screened *À nous la liberté* for Chaplin 'at least a dozen times'. But even if this were true, and no corroboration followed, the dehumanisation of the worker by the machine was an idea already general in the culture; it belonged to no one.

Tobis's case would have died with World War II, were it not for the animosity the United States Justice Department held for Chaplin. It was a United States court that extended the plaintiff's time from 1941 to 1943. In May of 1947, with Tobis having merged with 'Films Sonal', the case was renewed in France.

By now, Chaplin was under siege by McCarthyist elements in America, and the Chaplin studios paid to settle: $5,000 and 2.5 million francs. No court ever ruled against Chaplin, nor, David Robinson notes, has any court document ever emerged that sheds light on the motive of the German company Tobis for pursuing Chaplin with such relentlessness from the midst of the Nazi regime to the post-war Occupation.

One of Chaplin's lawyers would remark that Tobis, although it was registered in France, was 'really a German Nazi company'. Chaplin seemed so dangerous to Nazis and Americans alike that those who pursued this suit were willing even to overlook Clair's own negative portrayal of capitalism. Clair portrayed capitalism as a system shadowed by gangster elements, and Clair's factory owner, Louis, becomes a prey to organised crime. Given the continuation of the suit after the war, when supposedly the Germans could no longer, at least publicly, hold *The Great Dictator* against Chaplin, it seems apparent that the German suit was ancillary to the enormous effort well under way in the United States to disgrace Chaplin and deport him.

There was another lawsuit against *Modern Times.* A former Imperial soldier turned Bolshevik named Michael Kustoff sued Chaplin in federal court, also for plagiarism. Kustoff argued that Chaplin had stolen from his self-published autobiography of a man driven mad by conflicts with capitalism. He too had ended up in the prison ward of a hospital where he was visited by a minister and his wife. This nuisance suit was thrown out of court, but not until November 1939.

. . . .

A young J. Edgar Hoover, 1922

Chaplin's FBI file, opened on 15 August 1922, was labelled 'Communist Activities' on the ground that Chaplin had hosted a party for the Communist William Z. Foster. In 1922 and 1923, sympathising with the poor and the outcast seemed to people with far more formal education than Charles Chaplin to place them in a natural alliance with the Communist Party. That Chaplin supported socialist and Communist causes alike, that he provided personal encouragement and financial support to the front organisations of the Party, are a matter of public record.

In 1922, union organisers were already approaching Chaplin for contributions, including the then striking railroad workers, a fact noted by A. A. Hopkins, the FBI agent then in charge of reporting on Chaplin's activities. A 1924 report finds Chaplin sympathetic to the IWW, 'hiring many of them to work on his movie sets'.

Chaplin's offences, according to the FBI, included his ridicule of movie censor Will Hays, President of the Motion Picture Producers and Distributors of America, ever in search of 'seditious propaganda' in movies. From the start, Chaplin was indeed guilty of failing to endorse the status quo, and of satirising the inhumanity of capitalism. He worked as an artist, he believed, under the protection of the first amendment, which granted everyone the right to their views, however repellent they might be to those in power.

'We are against any kind of censorship and particularly against Presbyterian censorship,' Chaplin had laughed at Hays, putting a sign, 'Welcome Will Hays', over the door of the men's toilet in his studio. Hays was absurd, Chaplin suggested, with his edicts about what could and could not be shown in films. Most ridiculous was Hays's dictum that no toilet be pictured in any movie.

Meanwhile, the FBI, ever on the alert for 'Communist propaganda in the film industry', and with scant regard for the Constitutional protection of free speech, perceived Chaplin as unreliable. Movies, the FBI noted in Chaplin's file, had the power to alter the consciousness of the viewer, and, 'in view of the effect which such pictures will have upon the minds of the people of this country', perceived as its duty to stop Charles Chaplin. Among the FBI's tactics was to attack Chaplin as a Jew, and so appeal to then prevalent American anti-Semitism. Chaplin's real name was 'Israel Thornstein', the FBI decided. He spoke 'with a Jewish accent' too.

The FBI was joined by the Nazis who, in a propaganda tract of photographic portraits of Jews, included Chaplin's picture with the caption, 'this little Jewish tumbler, as disgusting as he is boring'. So the FBI and the Nazis shared and made use of the same disinformation.

When he was asked publicly if he was Jewish, Chaplin indignantly refused to deny this falsehood. Finally, questioned directly, he provided his answer: 'I do not have the honor.'

During World War II, terming himself 'a patriot of humanity' and a 'citizen of the world, neither a Democrat, a Republican or a Communist', Chaplin spoke on behalf of the Communist Party's front organisations, Russian War Relief, and the National Council of American-Soviet Friendship among them, even as he repeatedly distanced himself from the official Stalinist line. He spoke of the need to open a second front against Hitler (which was finally accomplished in 1944 on D-Day) and praised both 'the valiant Soviet people and our own ill-housed, ill-clad and ill-nourished', connecting all those suffering and in need.

At the same time, Chaplin said he stood for 'evolutionary change', hardly a paean to the Bolshevik revolution. 'The Communists are ordinary people like ourselves,' he insisted, and referred to the 'awakening of the Negro masses'; at the time the Communist Party was at the forefront of the few civil rights efforts that were attempted in the United States.

'There is a good deal of good in Communism,' Chaplin said in 1943 when the United States and the Soviet Union were allies. 'We can use the good and segregate the bad.' He added, 'I am not a Communist. I am just a clown.' Chaplin dined on a Soviet ship while US Customs men hovered nearby. 'Oh, I see we are under the power of the American Gestapo,'

Chaplin remarked, and this comment found its way into his FBI file. Chaplin couldn't help but note that 'the moment you try to tell the people the truth about life we run up against censorship'. He exposed the limits of American democracy. Mistakenly, at a moment decidedly not to his credit, he did defend the purges rampant in the Soviet Union. 'We are no longer shocked by Russian purges,' he said.

Only in 1943, more than twenty years after the FBI had opened its file, did Chaplin discover how directly and thoroughly they were stalking him. He learned that the Bureau was making inquiries about his relationship with Paulette Goddard, who had lived with him as his wife; ambiguity persists as to whether Chaplin and Goddard ever actually married. As naive as Chaplin, Goddard advised Chaplin to go directly to J. Edgar Hoover and demand to know what those 'bastards' were doing investigating him.

He should buy a $1 million war bond 'strictly for the publicity', the FBI writes that Goddard told Chaplin. That he had campaigned for Americans to buy war bonds during World War I was a fact inconvenient to the FBI's efforts against him. In 1943, the Los Angeles agent in charge of Chaplin's case, R. B. Hood, told Hoover that 'Chaplin very definitely is an artist and has been recognized as such all over the world'. It didn't matter.

The FBI enlisted the Internal Revenue Service (IRS) in monitoring Chaplin's bank accounts. The CIA (Central Intelligence Agency) reported on him to the FBI. By February 1945, a bill had been introduced in the United States Senate calling for Chaplin's deportation for 'Communist affiliations'.

Enlisted against him was the fact that he had never become an American citizen. Chaplin replied that he was 'a citizen of the world', not a nationalist. 'I don't believe in making any division of peoples,' he repeated. 'Citizenship papers don't mean a thing.' He pointed out that in America he was 'a paying guest'. Pressed, he argued that he paid taxes in the United States even on the considerable income he earned outside the country. Chaplin thought that income amounted to three-quarters of the total.

The Chaplin case reveals not least how effectively the Bureau had created assets of people presenting themselves as independent members of the press. A New York *Daily News* columnist and popular television personality, Ed Sullivan, on whose variety programme the Beatles were to make their first American television appearance, blasted Chaplin for belonging to 'at least five Communist front organizations'. Sullivan was vociferous in his attacks on Chaplin. 'Under our democracy, there are no "little people",' he ranted. 'Is you or is you ain't our baby? Are you with Uncle Sam or against him?'

Chaplin read one of Theodore Dreiser's poems at Dreiser's funeral and this too found its way into his file. For the FBI, Dreiser, the author of *An American Tragedy* and *Sister Carrie*, was not among the greatest of American novelists, as he most assuredly was, but a traitorous Communist.

Chaplin defied the FBI: 'I want a change and don't want the old rugged individualism ... rugged for a few, ragged for many,' he said during World War II. He contributed to a strike by the San Joaquin farm workers, although the strike relief committee was run by a member of the Communist Party, Ella Winter.

Like his Little Fellow, Chaplin refused to be either silent or passive. He sent a telegram to Pablo Picasso, urging that he lead a protest of French artists and march to the American Embassy in Paris to protest the deportation from the United States of composer Hanns Eisler. Eisler had trained as a composer under Arnold Schoenberg, and had worked with Bertolt Brecht; in exile from the Nazis in Hollywood, he was twice nominated for an Academy Award, for Fritz Lang's anti-Nazi film, *Hangmen Also Die* (1943) and for Clifford Odets's *None But the Lonely Heart* (1944). Eisler was working on music for the re-release of Chaplin's *The Circus* when the House Un-American Activities Committee closed in on him.

Interviewed by James Fay of the Catholic War Veterans, a virulent McCarthy ally clothed as a reporter, Chaplin reiterated his support for the composer. Eisler was 'a fine artist and a great musician and a very sympathetic friend', Chaplin said.

'Would it make any difference if he were a Communist?' Fay persisted.

'No, it wouldn't,' Chaplin said.

The FBI took note of Chaplin's efforts on behalf of Eisler, which had included that communication with Pablo Picasso. For the FBI, Picasso was no better than a 'French Communist'. Chaplin had become 'a dangerous alien' and an 'enemy of American principles', and there were few possessing the courage to argue otherwise.

In the post-war years, Chaplin's file was treated as a security matter. In defiance, at a 1947 press conference, Chaplin declared, 'Proceed with the witchhunt!' He repeated that underlying his work was 'a great sympathy for the underdog', and this applied even to Monsieur Verdoux, who turns to murder only after he loses his three-decade-long job as a bank clerk in the economic collapse of the 1929 Depression. Chaplin's insistence that he was 'for the little man' rendered him dangerous, a danger exacerbated by his abiding popularity, which allowed him to express ideas, among them the abiding ideal of economic equality, which were then and now, more often than not, casualties of self-censorship.

Stepping up his efforts to destroy Chaplin, in 1947 Hoover fed an article from *Pravda* to Hollywood gossip columnists Louella Parsons and Hedda Hopper. This article praised Chaplin as 'the greatest of all film actors', asserting that his films, despite their 'partylessness ... can and must be considered ours'. Chaplin was 'an old member of the Socialist Party of America', *Pravda* decided, perhaps with an eye toward refuting the charge that Chaplin was a member of the American Communist Party. Chaplin continued to deny that he had ever joined any political organisation.

The FBI also told its media assets that during the war Chaplin had a large quantity of rationed meat and cheese in his freezer. This too found its way into print. In her column, Hopper broadcast her friendship with J. Edgar Hoover, referring to him as 'Eddie'. By now Chaplin 'despise[d] the press' which had always 'lied about me. They have tried to build me up as a monster'.

With scant regard for the law, FBI agents made 'confidential searches' of the homes of Party members and fellow travellers, scanning their address books for Chaplin's name. They stole subscription lists from magazines like *New Masses*, hoping to discover Chaplin's name – and succeeded. They installed illegal wiretaps in the hotel rooms of Chaplin's friends. When his Communist Party membership could not be corroborated, the Bureau opened its own second front, attempting to defeat Chaplin on morals charges.

The FBI papered his file, which grew to nearly two thousand pages, with articles by left-wing critics. One, by Arnaud D'Usseau in *Mainstream*, praises Chaplin as 'our great artist', 'clear-sighted and fearless about most of the shamelessly naked contradictions in capitalist society', his films suffused with the 'spirit of revolt'. The FBI then investigated Chaplin for 'Soviet espionage activities'.

Through rumour, hearsay, and through breathtaking disinformation, Chaplin had been accused by a 'confidential source' of conspiring to purchase revolvers, machine guns and rifles, which were stored at 'an undisclosed address on Ventura Boulevard'. Chaplin and a partner, whose name is redacted on the document, supposedly had 'six airplanes that they are presently utilizing to fly these arms and other war materials in and out of Mexico'. Demonstrable proof was not forthcoming.

In April 1948, Chaplin sat down for an interview with the Immigration and Naturalization Service people (INS). Chaplin's honesty at once distanced him from the 'parlor pinks', more often than not reticent about how their lifestyles did not match their views. Many Party members denied their membership. Those like Dashiell Hammett, who were Party members without official membership, kept silent about their loyalties, although their defence of the Hitler–Stalin Pact and, earlier, of Stalin's show trials, made clear their relationship to the Soviet Union.

'I have about $30,000,000 worth of business,' Chaplin said, 'what am I talking about Communism for?' He termed the Hitler–Stalin Pact an 'outrage'.

'I don't like war and I don't like revolution,' Chaplin said. He did believe in 'unionism', and in the need to raise 'the standard of living of the American people'. This alone would prevent another Depression as well as preserve democracy. Once more Chaplin asserted, 'I have never belonged to any political organization.' Once more he denied that he had made financial contributions to the Communist Party. He had, however, bought half a million dollars worth of war bonds. He gave the INS nothing they could use against him. This would be the last time a government agency would subject itself to an interview with Charles Chaplin.

In 1948, the FBI prepared a Security Index card on Chaplin. The Bureau was assisted by the CIA, which filed a report about Chaplin on 23 July 1948. Yet, by December 1949, the FBI had to conclude, however reluctantly, that there was no evidence that Chaplin was a member of the Communist Party nor that he had contributed money to the Party.

On 7 February 1950, the Los Angeles field office recommended that the Chaplin case be closed: 'no information has been developed indicating that Chaplin has engaged in espionage activity or is so engaged at the present time'. After the INS experience, the FBI had to conclude that 'another interview with Chaplin himself would be entirely unproductive'.

The case would seem to have been closed when the FBI's most notorious informant, Louis F. Budenz, denounced Chaplin as a 'concealed Communist', and 'the equivalent of a member of the party'.

Monsieur Verdoux:
attacked by the
Communist Party as, in
contemporary parlance,
'politically incorrect'

New life was blown into Hoover's case. Budenz had been managing editor of the *Daily Worker*. Having seen the light, he now insisted that he himself had been required 'to defend the integrity of Chaplin, a Communist artist'. Budenz claimed to have heard a report that 'Chaplin had submitted the text of his moving picture *Modern Times* to the Moscow Board of Censorship in Russia and that he had changed certain sections of the production to conform to their criticism'. Budenz insisted that 'repeatedly' he had heard of Chaplin's 'financial aid to the Communist Party and to its fronts'.

Hoover now resumed his vendetta against Chaplin. He had to ignore the Communist Party's vehement objections to *Monsieur Verdoux* (1947) on the grounds that Chaplin had put his plea for peace in the mouth of a murderer, that the Party, Chaplin's supposed Communist admirers, were certainly not now defending his integrity as an artist.

Budenz was soon joined in his charges against Chaplin by another Communist apostate, Paul Crouch, who added to the FBI's legend about Chaplin that he was 'a devoted and loyal member of the Party', but had been ordered to 'remain a member at large'. The FBI's case was reopened.

Until the advent of Budenz and Crouch, Chaplin had attempted to ignore the gathering storm of FBI harassment. In 1949, he had permitted the Westland School, a progressive institution, to show *Modern Times* at a fundraiser. But when the Communist Party wanted to screen *The Circus* in July 1950 to benefit *People's World*, the West Coast Communist Party newspaper, Chaplin had his lawyers threaten violation of copyright should the film be exhibited. The lawyers then telephoned the FBI and informed them that this had been done.

The FBI had to face the reality that, over the long tenure of its pursuit of Charles Chaplin, witnesses, like Special Agent A. A. Hopkins, had died. The FBI could not produce its source for the 1923 statement that Chaplin in 1922 had donated $1,000 to the Communist Party.

Hoover feared that Chaplin might escape the punishment the FBI planned for him. He might fly off to Russia. He might flee to Mexico. 'Don't let this fellow do a run out,' Hoover wrote. The INS dutifully instructed border agents at El Paso, Seattle and San Diego to watch for Chaplin should he attempt to leave the country.

Hoover then opened his own second front. The vague charges of Communist Party membership, the slander about espionage – all of these collided with sticky first amendment issues. With the co-operation of the Justice Department, as Hoover's tail always wagged that dog, Hoover chose instead to engineer Chaplin's deportation on the grounds of 'moral turpitude'. Through a series of nasty federal trials, Chaplin was accused of violating a 1910 law, the 'Mann Act', which had been written to address the 'white slave' traffic. The Mann Act prohibited the transport of women across state lines for immoral purposes, namely prostitution. Chaplin had, inadvisedly, provided railroad tickets for a frantic young lover named Joan Barry (sometimes known as 'Berry'), and her mother, both to and from Los Angeles.

The law was then twisted to suggest that Chaplin, in assisting Barry's travel, had violated the Mann Act, as if he were the head of a prostitution ring. Chaplin had 'floated' Barry out of the state, the FBI charged, no matter that Barry had gone off to seek solace and financial help from another of her admirers, J. Paul Getty, the oilman. Soon Barry wandered back to Los Angeles, hardly a captive of a white slave or any other trade.

Chaplin was also accused of conspiring, financing and 'abetting' Barry in two 'criminal abortions'. Even reactionary columnist Westbrook Pegler had to admit that these charges were 'bad business', that the Mann Act involved women being taken across state lines for the express purpose of prostitution, which was clearly not the case in the entirely legal relationship between Barry and Chaplin.

The FBI's campaign was compromised by the character of the victim. Joan Barry, whom Chaplin had indeed promised to help with her fledgling career, was known as promiscuous, alcoholic, violent, erratic and suicidal. Barry had been caught shoplifting, writing bad cheques and attempting to extort money from rich men, not least Getty. As the months passed, the FBI feared that 'Joan Barry might land in jail and our case would be ruined'.

Hoover persisted, his commitment to ruining Chaplin by now a full-fledged personal vendetta. 'We should get started now to get our phase of this case lined up,' he instructed his agents. The INS wanted to help and re-interview the FBI's confidential informants, but Hoover refused to name them. He relied entirely on Joan Barry herself. Barry recounted, preposterously, a story of how Chaplin had told her that he had been offered a position in Russia as a 'Commisar' and that he thought of 'going back [sic] to Russia'. It was a place where he had never been.

After Chaplin was acquitted on the Mann Act charges, hoping to find some ground for overturning the court's decision, the FBI interviewed jury members who had originally voted to find Chaplin guilty in the secret ballot. Barry was now pregnant. FBI agents stole a 'bluish-green capsule' from her bedside, and then analysed it in the infamous FBI lab in the hope of determining that it induced abortion. The capsule turned out to be a liver extract prescribed for anaemia. Attempting to befriend Barry, Hedda Hopper stole documents out of her purse.

After Barry gave birth to a daughter, with the encouragement of the Justice Department she sued Chaplin for child support, claiming that he was the father. Chaplin submitted to blood tests. FBI media plants spread the word that Chaplin had taken mysterious injections in an attempt to change his blood type and so avoid responsibility for paternity. The editor of the *Journal of the American Medical Association* had to inform the Bureau that this was not scientifically possible. Despite conclusive evidence that Chaplin could not have been the biological father, he lost the paternity suit. 'Justice has been done!' Barry exulted. For many years Chaplin paid child support for a child who was not his own.

The FBI's Chaplin file is padded with the babblings of butlers and maids, railroad porters and disgruntled Communists. Included as well are fervent letters to J. Edgar Hoover from puritanical-minded citizens with an obvious animosity toward foreigners. These zealots, so furious at

Chaplin, had been easily manipulated by the managed press into believing that Chaplin was a threat to the moral well-being of the United States. Charlie Chaplin's FBI file is a kitchen sink of innuendo, distortion, half-truths and self-righteous outrage. Chaplin is even blamed for Soviet plans for a series of screenings of his films at the 'House of Cinema Workers in Moscow'.

On 8 October 1952, Hoover asked Frank Wisner, head of the CIA's clandestine services, for 'any information concerning subject's activity that might come to your attention'. Before it was over, in its pursuit of Chaplin, the FBI had enlisted the assistance not only of the IRS, the INS and the CIA, but even of the ONI (Office of Naval Intelligence) and US Army Intelligence. All the while, the FBI's sources refused to allow their identities to be divulged. One informant pleaded that it would 'jeopardize the position of his company, as well as his own position of employment in the moving picture industry'.

Helplessly, the left attempted to defend Chaplin. Communist Party member playwright Clifford Odets said that 'Charlie is not a communist at all. He is an anarchist ... he'd be tossed out of Russia in two weeks if he ever got in there.' This, of course, was true.

That same October, *Pravda*'s New York correspondent also attempted to analyze the fervent attacks on Chaplin. He pointed to 'such outstanding films as *Modern Times* and *City Lights*', which had disclosed 'the ulcers and vices of the notorious "American way of life",' as well as to Chaplin's portrayal of 'the little man's tragedy in the American jungles of capitalism'. For the truth of this portrayal, Chaplin was driven out of the United States.

In 1952, he travelled to France for the opening of *Limelight* where *L'Humanité* defined him as 'the "little man" hunted down by the masters of American reaction'. In November 1952, *Démocratie Nouvelle* spoke of Chaplin's two-reelers as depicting 'the fight of man alone within a hostile environment, against the wheels of which are going over him, wheels against which it seems he can do nothing'. Chaplin's films 'symbolized the pain and the smile of the poverty-stricken', while 'his solitary march crossing the lower strata of his childhood gives us Charlie's dimensions'.

These French reviews found their way into Chaplin's FBI file as further evidence of his being a subversive. When Chaplin was summoned by the House Un-American Activities Committee, he announced that he planned to testify dressed in his tramp costume. The Committee changed its mind and decided that he would not be required to go to Washington after all.

Denying the Justice Department the pleasure of examining him on 'the desirability of his re-entering the country', denying the FBI the victory of determining whether 'he is admissible under the laws of the United States', laws the FBI itself violated at every turn, Charles Chaplin sailed into exile on 17 September 1952. Reporters with him on board the *Queen Elizabeth* inquired whether Chaplin had a message for the American public.

'Goodbye!' Chaplin said.

His wife, Oona, returned to the United States to close out what was reported to be a $5 million bank account. That same year, Joan Barry's mother had her committed to a mental institution 'as a schizophrenic or person with dual personality'.

Chaplin took up residence in Switzerland, where US intelligence agents opened and read his mail. The FBI's media assets continued to attack him. Writing in December 1953 in *The American Legion Magazine*, Victor Lasky chastised Chaplin for making the police 'a butt of his humour'. Chaplin was 'a fellow-traveler of communism', Lasky wrote, following the Budenz script. Lasky also chided Chaplin for not having become an American citizen.

A King in New York –
Chaplin chooses exile:
'It's too crazy here!'

The United States Attorney General James P. McGranery repeated that Chaplin had been 'publicly charged with being a member of the Communist Party, with grave moral charges, and with making statements that would indicate a leering, sneering attitude toward a country whose hospitality has enriched him', as if Chaplin's crime were his comedy itself. McGranery refrained from noticing that Chaplin had broken no law.

In 1957, in *A King in New York*, Chaplin reprised his American fate. A deposed King, an unlikely Communist, Charlie is harassed for his liberal desire that atomic power be enlisted for the common good rather than for military purposes. Throughout this underrated, quite startling and penetrating satire, there are autobiographical clues.

At the beginning reporters twice request that the King 'say a few words to the American people', as Chaplin had been asked to do. This time, Chaplin has a ready answer, if one laden with irony. He says he was deeply moved by the 'warm friendship and hospitality' he received in the United States, even as he is fingerprinted in the same scene.

A nightclub skit bears a close resemblance to the hilarious wallpaper-hanging scene in Chaplin's 1915 two-reeler, *Work*. Chaplin's son Michael, playing a young genius, demands, 'Do you have to be a Communist to read Marx?' He has no 'aspiration' to write for women's magazines, the King says, even as Chaplin wrote that series for *Woman's Home Companion* in the early 30s.

By the end of *A King in New York*, accused of being a foreign conspirator in the pay of Communists, the King, Chaplin's surrogate, is all too ready to return to Europe. That he has been 'cleared of Communism' is not enough to keep him in America. 'It's too crazy here!' he decides. 'I'll sit it out in Europe', as, indeed, Chaplin did, with only one brief return to the United States to accept an absurdly belated honorary Academy Award. André Bazin would see *Monsieur Verdoux* as the logical extension of society's murderous treatment of the tramp in *Modern Times*, of America's outrageous condemnation of Charles Spencer Chaplin.

Respectability pursued Charles Chaplin in his exile. In 1962, he received an honorary Doctor of Letters degree from Oxford University, he who had never gone beyond the fourth grade of school, if that. The irony was vivid. England was the place where, as Chaplin had said in his 1931 visit to London, 'nobody ever cared for me or wanted me'.

At Oxford, he sat opposite bellicose Dean Rusk, John F. Kennedy's Secretary of State, who was forced to listen to Chaplin being described as a man who 'sympathizes with the underdog'. The *New York Times* now urged that the ban against Chaplin, if it still existed, be lifted: 'we do not believe the Republic would be in danger'. Queen Elizabeth II knighted Charles Chaplin on 2 January 1975.

And still the FBI was not done. The Bureau maintained its security file on Chaplin even after his death when his body was stolen from its resting place.

Chaplin's legend outlived him, erasing the FBI's thirty-year effort to consign him to oblivion. Chaplin's reputation as a film artist soared. Those who had insisted that Buster Keaton or Harold Lloyd, Chaplin's avowed imitator, had bested him retreated before critical wisdom with respect to Chaplin's considerable contribution to the art of the cinema.

In the 1990s, Andrew Sarris called Chaplin 'the single most important artist produced by the cinema'. Through comedy, Chaplin penetrated to the core of how social injustice deforms the psyches of ordinary people. James Agee called the tramp 'the most humane and most nearly complete among the religious figures our time has evolved'. This is no less true than Eisenstein's comment in his essay, 'Charlie The Kid', that Chaplin had 'eyes able to see in the forms of merriment an Inferno as fierce as Dante's'.

Penetrating the miasma of the FBI's relentless pursuit, audiences continued to welcome the tramp, his artefacts treasured. In December 2004 the bamboo cane Chaplin used in *Modern Times* sold at auction at Christie's in London for $91,800. More than any of his films, *Modern Times* reveals that Chaplin remained true to his own story, to the lonely poverty into which he was born. It was for this fidelity to the truth of his personal history, no less than to the stark historical realities and political implications of the Depression, for which 50s' America could not forgive him. The wider world, however, had long ruled otherwise.

CREDITS

. . . .

Modern Times

USA
1936

Director
Charlie Chaplin

©Charles Chaplin
Production Company
Charles Chaplin Film
Corporation

Assistant Director
Carter DeHaven
Written by
Charlie Chaplin
Photographed by
Rollie Totheroh
Ira Morgan
Settings by
Charles D. Hall
Russell Spencer
Music Composed by
Charlie Chaplin
Music Conducted by
Alfred Newman
Music Arranged by
Edward Powell
David Raksin
Music Recorded by
Paul Neal
Frank Maher
*Use of popular musical numbers
by special permission*
Sound System
Westrex Electric Noiseless
Recording

[uncredited]
Producer
Charlie Chaplin
**General
Production Manager**
Alfred Reeves
**Assistant
Production Manager**
Jack Wilson

Assistant Director
Henry Bergman
Script Clerk
Della Steele
Casting Director
Allan Garcia
Process Photography
Bud Thackery
Assistant Camera
Mark Marlatt
Ted Minor
Morgan Hill
Gaffer
Don Donaldson
Portrait Photography
Max Munn Autrey
Editor
Charlie Chaplin
Art Director
Danny Hall
**Make-up for
Charlie Chaplin and
Paulette Goddard**
Elizabeth Arden
Props
Hal Atkins
Bob Depps
Purchasing Agent
Joe Van Meter
Projectionist
Garwood Averill

Cast
Charlie Chaplin
a factory worker
Paulette Goddard
a gamin
Henry Bergman
a café proprietor
Stanley Sandford
burglar/Big Bill
Chester Conklin
a mechanic
Hank Mann
burglar
Stanley Blystone
Sheriff Couler
Allan Garcia
President
of Electro Steel Corp
Dick Alexander
a convict

Cecil Reynolds
the chaplain
Myra McKinney
the chaplain's wife
Murdoch McQuarrie
Wilfred Lucas
Ed Le Sainte
Fred Malatesta
Sam Stein
Juana Sutton
Ted Oliver

[uncredited]
Louis Natheaux
burglar/the addict
Gloria De Haven
extra

10 reels
87 minutes

The British Board of Film
Classification records that the
version of the film passed for
UK audiences on 6 February
1936 ran 8,081 feet/89 minutes
5 seconds

Black and White

**Filmed between October
1934 and November
1935 in Los Angeles and
San Pedro (California)**

US distributor
United Artists Corp.
New York première
5 February 1936
Los Angeles première
12 February 1936
General release
21 February 1936

Credits checked by
Julian Grainger

BIBLIOGRAPHY

Agee, James, *Agee on Film: Volume I*. (New York: The Universal Library: Grosset & Dunlap, 1969).

Atkinson, Brooks, 'Beloved Vagabond: Charlie Chaplin Canonized out of a Sentimental Memory Book,' *The New York Times*, 16 February 1936, I, p. X1.

Bazin, André, 'Charlie Chaplin', in Hugh Gray (ed.), *What Is Cinema?: Vol. 1* (Berkeley and Los Angeles: University of California Press, 1967).

————, 'The Myth of Monsieur Verdoux', '*Limelight*, or the Death of Molière', 'The Grandeur of *Limelight*', in Hugh Gray (ed.), *What Is Cinema?: Vol. 2* (Berkeley, Los Angeles and London: University of California Press, 1972).

Bergan, Ronald. *Sergei Eisenstein: A Life in Conflict* (Woodstock, NY: The Overlook Press, 1999).

Chaplin, Charles. FBI File. Department of Justice. Subject: Charlie Chaplin. File Number: 100–127090. Available from the Federal Bureau of Investigation. Freedom of Information/Privacy Acts Section.

Chaplin, Charles, *My Trip Abroad* (New York: Harper and Brothers, 1922).

————, 'A Comedian Sees the World', *Woman's Home Companion* vol. 61, (September 1933–January 1934). Five-part memoir.

————, *My Autobiography* (New York: Simon and Schuster, 1964).

'Chaplin Gibes at Leaders', *New York Times*, 14 June 1932, p. 26.

'Chaplin Plans New Film', *New York Times*, 29 August 1933, p. 20.

'Chaplin's Forthcoming Comedy', *New York Times*, 19 August 1934, I, p. X3.

'Chaplin Film Here Jan. 16', *New York Times*, 18 December 1934, I, p. 32.

'Chaplin's *Modern Times*', *New York Times*, 17 November 1935, Section 9, p. 5.

'Enter Charles Chaplin, Tardily', *New York Times*, 2 February 1936, I, p. X5.

'Chaplin Premiere to Be Held Tonight', *New York Times*, 5 February 1936, I, p. X5.

'Chaplin Fans Jam Block At Opening', *New York Times*, 6 February 1936, I, p. 23.

'London Welcomes New Chaplin Film', *New York Times*, 12 February 1936, I, p. 25.

Churchill, Douglas W., 'Hollywood Letter: The Studios Embark on a Spending Spree – Six Pictures for Mr Chaplin', *New York Times*, 15 September 1935, I, p. X3.

D.W.C., 'The Curious Mr Chaplin: A Bundle of Paradoxes, the Comedian Is Still a Riddle to the Film World', *New York Times*, 16 February 1936, I, p. X1.

Eisenstein, Sergei, 'Charlie the Kid', in Jay Leyda (ed.), *Film Essays and a Lecture* (New York: Praeger, 1970).

————, *Immoral Memories: An Autobiography*, trans. by Herbert Marshall (Boston, MA: Houghton Mifflin Company, 1983).

Gehring, Wes D., 'Chaplin and the Progressive Era: The Neglected Politics of a Clown', *Indiana Social Studies Quarterly* vol. 34, Autumn 1981, pp. 10–18.

Jacobs, Lewis, 'Charles Chaplin: Individualist', in *The Rise of the American Film: A Critical History* (New York: Teachers College Press, 1968).

Kitchen, Karl K., 'Chaplin and "The Masses"', *New York Times*, 17 March 1935, Section 9, p. 4.

Maland, Charles J., *Chaplin and American Culture: The Evolution of a Star Image* (Princeton, NJ: Princeton University Press, 1989).

Milton, Joyce, *Tramp: The Life of Charlie Chaplin* (New York: HarperCollins, 1996).

Montagu, Ivor, *With Eisenstein in Hollywood* (New York: International Publishers, 1969).

Newhouse, Edward, 'Charlie's Critics', *Partisan Review and Anvil* vol. 3, April 1936, i, 25–6.

'N. Y. Critics and Chaplin', *Variety*, 12 February 1936, p. 4. See also '*Modern Times*', signed Abel. Ibid., p. 16.

Nugent, Frank S., 'Heralding the Return, after an Undue Absence, of Charlie Chaplin in *Modern Times*', *New York Times*, 6 February 1936, I, p. 23.

————, 'The Reign of Good King Charlie', *New York Times*, 9 February 1936, I, p. X5.

Potamkin, Harry Alan, *The Compound Cinema: The Film Writings of Harry Alan Potamkin*, ed. Lewis Jacobs (New York: Teachers College Press, 1977).

Ramsaye, Terry, 'Chaplin Ridicules Reds'
Claim Film Aids Cause', *Motion Picture
Herald*, 7 December 1935, pp. 13–14.

Robinson, David, *Chaplin: His Life and Art*
(New York: McGraw-Hill, 1985).

Rozas, Lorenzo Turrent, 'Charlie Chaplin's
Decline', *Living Age*, June 1934, pp. 319–23.
Translated from *ruta*, a Communist literary
monthly (Mexico).

Sarris, Andrew, 'In the Wink of a Mustache',
review of *Charlie Chaplin* by John McCabe.
New York Times Book Review, 14 May 1978,
p. 4.

————, 'Charles Chaplin', in Richard Roud
(ed.), *Cinema: A Critical Dictionary: The
Major Film-makers. Volume One* (New York:
Viking Press, 1993), pp. 201–12.

Shumyatsky, B., 'Charlie Chaplin's New
Picture', *New Masses*, 24 September 1935,
pp. 29–30. Trans. by Leon Dennen. This
article appeared originally in *Pravda*
(Moscow).

Tyler, Parker, *Chaplin: Last of the Clowns* (New
York: The Vanguard Press, 1948).

Von Wiegand, Charmion, 'Little Charlie, What
Now?' *New Theater* vol. 3, March 1936,
pp. 6–13.

ALSO PUBLISHED

If you would like further information about future BFI Film Classics or about other books on film, media and popular culture from BFI Publishing, please write to:

BFI Film Classics
BFI Publishing
21 Stephen Street
London W1T 1LN